D1566787

Disasters &c.

The Maritime World of
Marblehead 1815–1865

PLAN
OF
MARBLEHEAD
MASS.
FROM ACTUAL SURVEY
By H. McINTIRE, C. E. &c.
1850.
Published by HENRY McINTIRE N.E. Corner of Perry & Pine Sts.

Scale of Feet

Disasters &c.

THE MARITIME WORLD OF
MARBLEHEAD 1815–1865

JOHN R. H. KIMBALL

PETER E. RANDALL PUBLISHER LLC
Portsmouth, New Hampshire 03802

2005

Copyright © 2005 John R. H. Kimball
All Rights Reserved

Copies are available from:
www.disastersetc.com

Published by:
Peter E. Randall Publisher LLC
Portsmouth, New Hampshire 03802
www.perpublisher.com

Design:
Grace Peirce

ISBN: 1-931807-36-1

Library of Congress Control Number: 2005924424

Contents

PREFACE

THE EARLY HISTORY OF THE MASSACHUSETTS TOWN OF MARBLEHEAD as the preeminent fishing port of the New World, and the exploits of its citizens on land and sea during the Revolution and the War of 1812, have been often recounted. Less well known are its maritime activities after the latter war through the Civil War. This period saw the final flowering of its fishing fleet, its sea captains, and its shipbuilding.

This book describes the unique nature of Marblehead's maritime commerce during this period through the careers of its fishermen, sea captains, and shipowners, and the words of contemporaries. — What was it like? How did it work? — Fishing reached a peak, and then declined; Marblehead sea captains such as Josiah P. Creesy, Jr., of the clipper ship *Flying Cloud*, established standards of speed and perseverance on the high seas; Marbleheader Joseph Story established maritime law in the United States as a Justice of the Supreme Court; and seven large sailing ships, including three clipper ships, were built in Marblehead and sent throughout the world during the explosive rise and fall of shipping known as the clipper ship era. The book's title refers to the maritime column in most daily newspapers during this period headed "Disasters &c.," which listed the accidents that had befallen vessels, including many mentioned in this narrative.

The author is indebted to many for help. He began with a few documents inherited from Marblehead ancestors, but these were soon eclipsed by the resources of the Marblehead Museum and Historical Society and the Peabody Essex Museum, and ship registries, litigation reports, newspapers, ships' logs, and other original sources in a variety of places. In Marblehead, he is particularly grateful to Maureen Graves Anderson, Robert Booth, Daniel Dixey, Richard Bridgeo, and Karen MacInnis of the Marblehead Museum and Historical Society.

Lincoln, Massachusetts, 2005

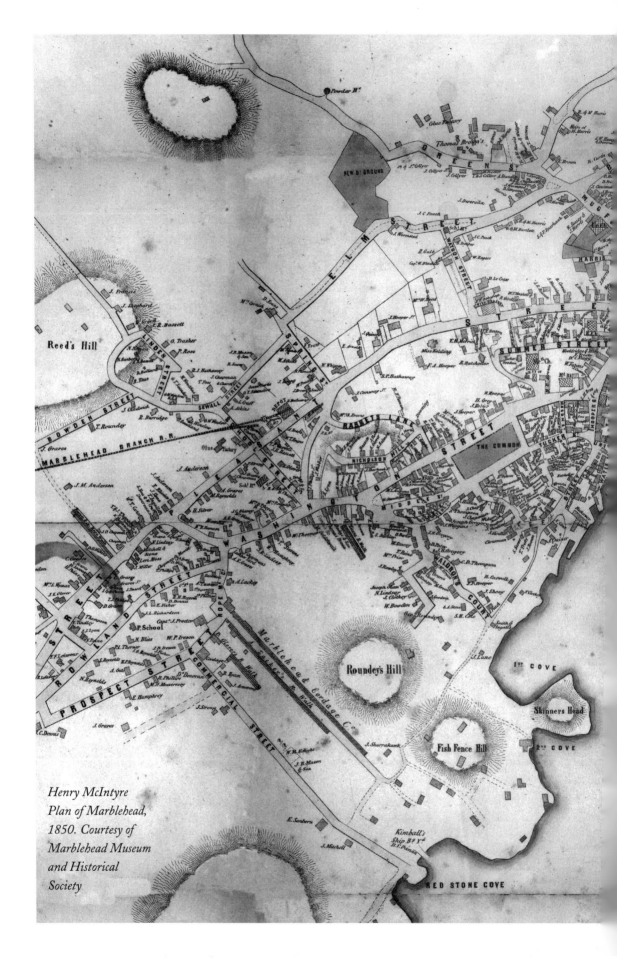

Henry McIntyre
Plan of Marblehead,
1850. Courtesy of
Marblehead Museum
and Historical
Society

DRYING FISH, LITTLE HARBOR.

From Harpers New Monthly Magazine, July 1874, page 197

ONE

MARBLEHEAD

$\mathcal{F}$ISHERMEN WERE ATTRACTED TO MARBLEHEAD originally by its harbors, located on the coast of Massachusetts roughly fifteen miles north of Boston. Settlement began in the early 17th century at Little Harbor, primarily by fishermen from England and France.[1] Settlement then spread to the Great Harbor, some $^1/_2$ mile wide and 1.5 miles long, which protected their vessels from all winds except northeasters. The settlers used the steep, rocky headlands, not really suitable for farming, to dry their salt cod.

The town's prosperity grew in the 18th century as the fishermen began to export their fish directly to markets in Europe and the West Indies, rather than through middlemen in neighboring Salem and in Boston.[2] Throughout this period, Marblehead shipped more dried codfish than all the rest of New England together, and, at the time of the Revolution, it was the third busiest port in Massachusetts after Salem (first) and Boston.[3] Nurtured in the rugged fishing life, Marbleheaders were important participants in the Revolutionary War, on both land and sea.[4] Colonel Azor Orne of Marblehead, a member of the Continental Congress and of the state and federal Constitutional Conventions, described the extent of the colonial Marblehead codfishery in a letter to General Benjamin Lincoln, and stated that, if fishing rights were taken away in the peace negotiations following the Revolution, "I should be for continuing the war until there was no men left" (see Appendix A).[5]

Thanks to the insistence of Azor Orne, John Adams, and others, the treaty ending the Revolutionary War provided that "the people of the United States shall continue to enjoy unmolested the right to take fish of every kind on the Grand Bank, and on the other banks of Newfoundland; also in the Gulph of Saint Lawrence, and at all other places in the sea where the inhabitants of both countries used at any time heretofore to fish."[6] The codfisheries of Marblehead became most profitable during the first six or eight years of the 19th century, and the number of schooners involved reached a peak of 116 in 1807 (Appendix B); the town's population reached 5,800 in 1810.[7]

The fishing industry was bottled up again by the embargo of 1807 and then by the War of 1812, brought on in reaction to the British impressment of American sailors and blockades. But many Marblehead vessels fitted out as privateers during the war, with commissions from the government to take enemy ships. As historian Samuel Eliot Morison says,

> Privateering was much the most popular form of service in maritime Massachusetts; it paid better wages, was safer, and more fun than the army or navy. Marblehead, which supported the war, provided 726 privateersmen, 120 naval seamen, and only 57 soldiers, not including the local militia.[8]

Some six hundred Marblehead privateersmen, most of the seafaring population of the town, became prisoners of war at some point, and most of them spent time in Dartmoor prison in Devonshire, England, until they were exchanged for British prisoners.[9] One among them, an ancestor of Nathaniel Hawthorne, described the Marbleheaders he met in a book that was edited by Hawthorne (who lived many years in Salem, next to Marblehead):

> Our first lieutenant was a fine specimen of a man, and of a sailor. He was a native of Marblehead, a town renowned in American history for the sturdy patriotism of its sons. He was a fine, well proportioned, man, of a frame capable of enduring the greatest fatigue, sinewy, and well knit; and his temper and disposition of the greatest placability and equanimity. Yet, there was no weakness about him, he was resolute and bold would state his orders with clearness and precision, and would insist on their being obeyed promptly and effectually.... During my privateering days, I saw much of these gallant sons of the ocean, and found them to be

> such sterling good fellows, notwithstanding their eccentricities—so full
> of the milk of human kindness—ever ready to share with those poorer
> than themselves, and to do a poor fellow a brotherly kindness—that I
> contracted such a respect for the character of a Marbleheadman, that it
> sticks to me yet.[10]

Though American privateers captured or destroyed 1,350 British ships, the
U.S. Navy was at best ambivalent about them because they diverted large numbers
of seamen and weakened the regular navy. But 80 of the crew of the U.S. frigate
Constitution were citizens of Marblehead, and its victory over the British frigate
Guerriere, on August 19, 1812, was for that reason considered almost a local victory
in Marblehead.[11] On Sunday, April 3, 1814, the *Constitution*, piloted by a Marbleheader (Samuel Green) and witnessed by crowds of townspeople, sailed into
Marblehead Harbor and under the protection of its forts to evade two pursuing
British frigates.[12] After the war, "hardly a dozen houses in the town were painted,
and ruin was the average condition, the broken window panes outnumbering the
whole ones."[13] The fishing industry recovered to a large extent, although the peace
treaty retrenched somewhat on the rights of Americans to fish along the coasts of
Newfoundland and Labrador.[14] Marblehead continued to be the principal codfishing town in America for half a century after the Revolution.

At various times, social commentators from outside Marblehead criticized
its inhabitants for failing to develop their town beyond the role of a fishing port,
calling Marbleheaders creatures of habit and lacking in ambition. For example,
the Congregational minister in neighboring Salem, William Bentley, wrote in his
diary in 1816,

> The many aged muscular men in Marblehead discovers the true
> character of their employment. No men endure fatigue longer, & have
> more presence of mind in danger, in things they propose & when under
> their own command. Such are their habits in the fishery. They have no
> other authority than from having the same habits & objects. They make
> often troublesome merchantmen, & they make awkward soldiers. But no
> men are equal to them in things which they know how to do from habit.
> None more persevering or so fearless.[15]

To these outsiders' eyes, Marblehead looked poor and smelled fishy (a smell
that Marbleheaders, however, considered "so strong and sweet that it is positively
agreeable").[16] Fishermen were described as

VIEW OF THE TOWN OF MARBLEHEAD, MASSACH

a race apart from those inhabitants of the country who draw their living from the mechanical arts, or the soil;—an effect of the peculiarities of character which grow out of the fisherman's profession, and the circumstances which inevitably attend it.… [The fisherman's] circle of art is the identical circle of his great grandfather … he is acquainted with exactly the same fishing banks, and exactly the same phenomena of tides and winds; he sails in a boat of the same rude construction, and employs implements that have undergone no change.

*View of the Town of Marblehead, Massachusetts.
From* Gleason's Pictorial VI (1854). *Courtesy of
the Peabody Essex Museum, Salem, Mass.*

This description—of Scottish fishermen by the Commissioners for the British Fisheries in 1842—might have been of Marblehead.[17] Marblehead's critics noted that, while Marblehead remained a fishing port, Salem had become a prosperous foreign-trading port. With more than twice the population and twice the land area of Marblehead, Salem had evolved from primarily a fishing port before the Revolutionary War to a very wealthy trading port between the wars, building ships and sending them to the Far East and throughout the world.[18] It was probably the richest American city per capita in 1790, and was a world apart from Marblehead, though only a few miles distant. Morison remarks,

> Across [Salem] harbor, obscuring the southerly channel, Marblehead presents her back side of rocky pasture to the world at large, and Salem in particular....
>
> Marblehead, a scant three miles from Salem, was as different in its appearance, its commerce, and the character of its people, as if it lay overseas.[19]

Marblehead also drew unfavorable comparisons with Beverly, on the other side of Salem, a more diverse town with a somewhat smaller population (4200 in 1830) and more than three times the land area of Marblehead.[20] Beverly reflected its Puritan roots by emphasizing outward appearances—Timothy Dwight, a Congregational divine and President of Yale, described the inhabitants of Beverly in the 1790s as "distinguished for good order, industry, sober manners, and sound morals," while describing Marbleheaders as "less industrious, economical, and moral, unless I am misinformed, than their neighbors in Salem and Beverly."[21] But these observers perhaps failed to appreciate the communal nature of the Marblehead codfishery, and the extent to which the town surpassed its rivals in productivity. Despite their supposed lack of industry, Marblehead fishermen dominated the codfishing industry, catching in 1834 (a good year for fish) about 160 quintals of cured fish per man/year (there are 112 pounds per quintal), compared to Beverly's 120 quintals per man/year, and lesser amounts for other ports.[22] The Marbleheaders were roughly a third more productive than their competitors, and they were twice as productive as the average Massachusetts fisherman had been a century earlier in smaller vessels closer inshore.[23] Even Morison rather grudgingly admitted that "[f]ishermen seem to have been a much happier and more independent class of seafarers than whalemen or merchant sailors."[24] And as we shall see, many men of Marblehead also became sea captains and shipowners engaged in foreign trade.

From the beginning, Marbleheaders said they had come to Marblehead to fish, not for religious freedom.[25] After two hundred years (and probably at least another hundred before that in the ports from which they came), these men and women, and the social environment that supported them, had been selected primarily for productivity in fishing, and those with less ability in this field had found other means of earning a living.

The character of Marbleheaders is perhaps best described by one of her native sons, Joseph Story (1779–1845), who would define maritime law in the United States as a member of the U.S. Supreme Court:

> The inhabitants of a town so situated, and especially of a town almost wholly engaged in the fisheries, whose voyages began and ended in the same port, and whose occupation when abroad is in sounding the depth of the ocean, and drawing their lines upon the stormy waves of the Banks of Newfoundland, have little variety in their thoughts or conversation. Their lives have few incidents but those perilous adventures which everywhere belong to a seafaring life. Their habits are necessarily plain, their morals pure, and their manners, if not rough, at least generally unpolished and unpretending....
>
> The people of Marblehead are a peculiar race; and as utterly unlike their neighbors as though they belonged to another age or country. The lines of their character are perhaps a little less marked than formerly, from their wider intercourse in later years with other places, but still they are deep and permanent, strong and full of meaning. They are a

generous, brave, humane, honest, straightforward people; sagacious in their own affairs, but not wise beyond them; confiding and unsuspecting; hospitable by nature, though stinted in means; with a love of home scarcely paralleled, and an indifference to the show and splendor of wealth, which cannot be easily imagined; frugal and laborious; content with their ordinary means, neither rejecting learning nor over anxious for its attainment. The very rocks of their shores, the very barrenness of the strand on which their buildings rest, the very scantiness of the mother soil on which they were born, and in which they expect to lie buried when they are dead, have to them an indescribable charm. They love it with an intensity of interest which neither time nor distance can control.[26]

Endnotes

1   The fishermen's provenance was diverse. Gray (1984) concludes—contrary to earlier theories that the first settlers came from the Channel Islands—that they likely came from the West Country of England. See Roads (1897) p. 7, *Vital Records of Marblehead* (1903, hereafter VRM), and Heyrman (1984), p. 214. An article in the *Marblehead Messenger* of May 27, 1904, called the Channel Island theory a "threadbare and probably unfounded tradition.... We doubt if a single Jersey or Guernsey name can be found in the annals of Marblehead prior to the year 1700.... Doubtless there was a strong and dominating immigration that came here from the Channel Islands and from Devonshire in the years following the revocation of the Edict of Nantes in 1685, and there are probably few of the old families of Marblehead who do not possess a dash of Gallic blood." By the time Louis Russell, a French Huguenot, arrived in Marblehead in 1717, there were already many of French descent living in Marblehead. Louis Russell genealogy, Marblehead Museum and Historical Society. See "A New Look at the Essex [County] 'French,'" David T. Koric, 110 Essex Institute Historical Collections, pp. 167 ff. (1974). The Isle of Jersey, though a British dependency, is only 14 miles off the coast of France, and many inhabitants had French names. Frenchmen may also have passed through Jersey on the way to the new world. It seems likely also that some of the early fishermen came to Marblehead from the British and French migratory fishery in the waters off Newfoundland. Marblehead fishermen continued to bring other fishermen from northern ports to Marblehead in the early 19th century (see below).

2   They were encouraged in this by Parson Barnard, Joseph Swett, and Robert "King" Hooper. See Bowden, and Lord and Gamage p. 69. Vickers (1994) emphasizes the rather grim economic imperatives in the development of Marblehead and other Essex County fishing communities in the 17th and 18th centuries: "Men who experienced the numbing cold of handlining for cod in subfreezing temperatures, the boredom of midsummer days spent shrouded in fog, and the fear of riding out a November gale in the blackness of night—all in the knowledge that their best efforts might not be rewarded with an adequate catch or a decent market—could easily have been drawn into other lines of work, had the opportunity existed." (p. 264).

3   See Bradlee (1929) p. 1 and McFarland (1911) p. 85. Drake writes (1875/6): "To quote from Douglass, he says: 'In 1746 Marblehead ships off more dried cod than all the rest of New England besides. Anno 1732 a good fish year, and in profound peace, Marblehead had about one hundred and twenty schooners of about fifty tons burden, seven men aboard, and one man ashore to make the fish, or about one thousand men employed, besides the seamen who carry the fish to market. Two hundred quintals considered a fare. In 1747 they have not exceeding seventy schooners, and make five

fares yearly to I. Sables, St. George's Banks, etc'" (p. 235). The Douglass he refers to is William Douglass. A "fare" means a voyage.

4   See Billias (1960) and Roads pp.196ff.

5   From the Turner file, Marblehead Museum and Historical Society. Azor Orne (1731–96) had also been a member of the Committee of Safety. General Lincoln had been in command of the part of the army that included the Marblehead regiment under Colonel John Glover. Roads pp. 100ff, 181, 267.

6   McFarland pp. 127 and 141.

7   Roads p. 303.

8   Morison (1921) p. 199. Maclay (1899) states: "Many of our privateersmen were men engaged in the Newfoundland fisheries, and a hardier or more daring set of men would be difficult to find. An American periodical, of the date August 8, 1812, notes: 'About thirty fishing vessels have arrived at Marblehead (Mass.), from the Banks within a few days, and only three remained absent. These hardy and patriotic citizens will generally become *fishers of ships*.'" (p. 14).

9   See Chadwick (1895); Roads, p. 318. Chadwick, born in Marblehead to a fishing family, became a Unitarian minister in Brooklyn, NY, and an author and poet. Roads pp. 428 and 448.

10 Browne (1846) chapter 3. Authorship has also been attributed to John Lord, brother of Nathaniel Hawthorne's grandmother, Miriam Lord Manning. Hawthorne was surveyor of the port at the Salem Custom House 1846–49.

11 George R. Clark *et al.* (1939) states: "By diverting large numbers of seamen, [privateering] weakened the regular navy; and as the results were far less than might have been secured by men-of-war, it seems from our point of view to have been of doubtful advantage….Privateering was profitable business to those who succeeded, and it must be admitted commercial instinct quite as often as patriotism was the impelling motive. There were about 500 of these vessels, and they captured or destroyed 1,350 British ships" (p. 201). See also Roads pp. 305, 310, and 314–15; Chadwick (1895).

12 It later sought the greater safety of Salem Harbor, farther inland.

13 Chadwick (1874).

14 Vickers (1994) p. 275; McFarland pp. 154, 48–49.

15 September 1816; vol. 4, p. 409. McFarland says of fishermen: "He was held fast-bound to the life on the sea by the chains of habit. The traditions of the family and the education of the children were confined chiefly to nautical affairs" (p. 151). See also Drake p. 243.

16 Chadwick (1874) p. 196. Captain Goelet stated in about 1750: "The greatest distaste a person has to this place is the stench of the fish, the whole air seems tainted with it. It may in short be said it's a Dirty, Erregular, Stincking Place" (*New England Historical and Genealogical Register*, 1870, p. 57, quoted in Drake p. 243).

17 "Report of the Commissioners for the British Fisheries of their Proceedings, 1842,"
    published as "Our Scottish Fishermen" in *The Living Age* 17 (September 7, 1844):
    291ff. The report noted: "The [female] sex occupy among the fisher population a
    much more prominent place than the humbler women of the country generally....
    [T]he profession of the fisherman furnishes employment, though not without long
    intervals of leisure, to the whole population of the fishing village, young and old....
    [O]ne curious effect of this employment of the very young, is a corresponding pre-
    cocity of development among the children of a fishing village.... In his sixteenth or
    seventeenth year, the growing lad accompanies his father to sea.... [H]e marries, ere
    he is turned of twenty, a girl of his own class, of eighteen.... There is no other portion
    of our ... population so eminently chaste as the inhabitants of our fishing villages."

18 Morison (1921) pp. 30 and 79ff.; "Salem Maritime," National Park Service.

19 Morison (1921) pp. 81, 138, and 311. Drake says: "If not insular, your genuine Mar-
    bleheader is the next thing to it. The rest of the world is merged with him into a place
    to sell his fish and buy his salt. Even Salem, Beverly, and the parts adjacent draw but
    little on his sympathy or his fellowship: in short, they are not Marblehead" (p. 244).

20 Vickers (1994), p. 194.

21 Dwight (1969) vol. 1, pp. 322 and 332. "For Dwight, external appearances, whether
    of people or of their houses and public buildings, reflected internal values" (Introduc-
    tion, p. xli). Morison and others repeated these criticisms based on hearsay (Morison,
    1921, pp. 140–41). See also Bourne (1989) p. 76. What Dwight actually observed was:
    "Marblehead, through which we passed merely for the sake of seeing it, is like Salem
    built on a peninsula, but more rough, rocky, and unpleasant than any which I have
    seen. The rocks are often very large and so thickly lodged on the surface that there
    seems to be hardly earth enough for the houses to stand on. On such ground regular-
    ity cannot be expected. The streets, or rather roads, wind where the rocks permit; the
    houses are built where the inhabitants can find room. The great body of the houses,
    belonging, as we concluded, to the fishermen, are ordinary and decayed. A few, the
    property, as we supposed, of their employers, are valuable buildings. The inhabitants,
    it will be remembered, suffered very severely during the Revolutionary War. The town
    made a better appearance to my eye in 1774 than in 1796" (vol. 1, p. 332). He also
    remarked with astonishment on the number of children in Marblehead. Of course,
    farming families also had large numbers of children, but they were not as visible,
    because not as densely settled. John Adams, in 1766, noted: "The streets are narrow
    and rugged and dirty, but there are some very grand buildings" (Drake p. 244).

22 Beverly was similar to Marblehead in focusing on the Grand Banks codfishery, and
    giving 3/8 of profits to the owner. She sent 43 schooners (many skippered and crewed
    by the Larcum and Woodbury families) to the Banks in 1834, only 17 of which were
    over 70 tons. They caught an average of 800 quintals per 6-man crew. Marblehead
    sent 58 schooners, only 13 of which were less than 70 tons. They caught an average

of 1,100 quintals per 6.5-man crew (compare also Gloucester with under 100 quintals per man/year, see chapter 5). The fishing agreements required by the bounty law show tonnage of vessel, names of crew, total quintals, and dates of fares (National Archives and Records Administration record group 036: 20/10/06-5 to 20/10/07-3, hereafter Fishing Agreements). The productivity figures are rough because sometimes not all the fishermen who signed an agreement fished all fares, and some who signed were boys who did not catch a full share of fish. Marblehead fishermen had also exceeded their Beverly counterparts' productivity in 1825, with 105 quintals per man/year versus 90. Marblehead had 77 schooners (35 under 70 tons) and Beverly 24 (11 over 70 tons), but several of the Beverly fishing agreements differed in form, and are now difficult to interpret. Fewer of the Marblehead schooners (63 of 77) went to the Grand Banks (based on the assumption that those making four or more fares per year must have fished closer to Marblehead), and those that did not go to the Grand Banks had smaller total catches. Excluding schooners with four or more fares, the Marblehead average was 117 quintals per man/year for 1825 versus 90 for Beverly, roughly the same one-third greater productivity per man as in 1834.

23 Vickers (1994), p. 154.

24 Historian Daniel Vickers (1995) says of the Newfoundland fishermen: "There is an ancient and deep-seated feeling among landward-oriented societies that fishing cultures tend to be backward and passive. Just as William Hubbard, a Puritan minister in New England, termed the fishermen of Massachusetts a 'dull and heavy-moulded sort of people' back in the seventeenth century, so the editors of an Icelandic fisheries journal could still refer to the fishing communities of his own country as havens of 'ignorance' and 'misunderstanding' in the middle of the twentieth century.... [H]owever, there is plenty of evidence to show that this is not the case. Indeed ... fishing people have always had agendas of their own—often quite at variance with those of fish merchants, government officials, and marine scientists" (pp. 2–3). No one in this period called Marbleheaders "dull and heavy-moulded"—quite the reverse. Cadigan describes the public discussion in Newfoundland in the period 1815–55 over other methods of fishing, such as seines and trawl lines. No evidence has been found of this discussion in Marblehead, but it doubtless occurred. "Fisheries and Maritime Collections," by the Cape Ann Historical Association, states: "Trawling was a European method of fishing long practiced on the Grand Bank by French and Canadian fishermen, but not attempted by Americans until the late 1840s.

25 Morison (1921) p. 13; Heyrman, p. 224.

26 Joseph Story (1851) pp. 32–33.

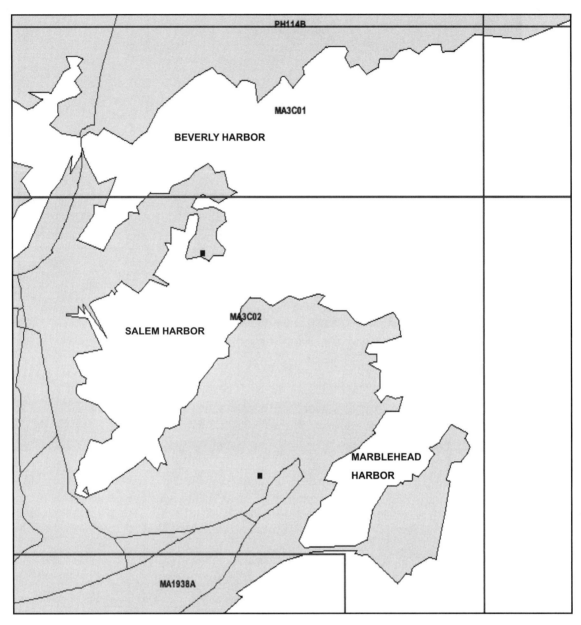

PH114B

MA3C01

BEVERLY HARBOR

SALEM HARBOR

MA3C02

MARBLEHEAD

HARBOR

MA1938A

U.S. Coast and Geodetic Survey Shoreline Survey

TWO

CODFISHING FROM MARBLEHEAD

LOADED WITH SUPPLIES FOR A THREE-MONTH VOYAGE, the 55-foot schooner *Garland* headed out from Marblehead to the Grand Banks off Newfoundland on its spring fare (voyage) on March 14, 1825. Samuel Snow was the 35-year-old skipper (as captains of fishing vessels were called), and he had put together a crew of four other men and two boys, but no cook.[1] This was Snow's first voyage in the *Garland*, but he had been fishing since he was a boy with his father and others, and had skippered the schooner *Joseph* the previous year. He was married to his second wife, Lucy Holmes, and had several children.[2] The *Garland* was owned by Edmund Kimball, and this was one of Kimball's first years sending out a number of fishing schooners. The association of Snow and his family with Kimball would continue for many years.

As another Marblehead sea captain recounts about a fishing voyage: "We passed Marblehead Rock and Half-way Rock, the latter near enough to enable each man to throw on it a few copper cents, for good luck, a custom religiously observed, in those days, by every Bank fisherman sailing from Marblehead...."[3] It took them the better part of a week to arrive at the Banks with a fair wind—schooners like the *Garland* were bluff-bowed and built for safety rather than speed, and the Grand Banks are about a third of the way to England.[4] Fishing was done by hand line, supplied by each fisherman, and continued day or night while the cod were biting, except for Saturday night to Sunday night. When the fish stopped biting, the fishermen changed their anchorage, and very occasionally, when supplies or repairs or help were needed, they would visit a Nova Scotia or Labrador port, "and according to their own account 'take possession of the town.'" Sometimes they would bring men from the port back to Marblehead.[5] But mostly, as long as the fish were biting it was fishing, day or night, fair weather or foul, until they had used up all the salt for preserving the fish, or were ready to return.

Fishing was hard work, even in decent weather. According to one observer:

> The hauling of fish over the rail of a vessel, with lines sixty or seventy feet long [or 300 feet on the Grand Banks], is by no means an easy task. When a halibut or large cod is attached to the line, it requires the man to put forth his whole strength, and sometimes the aid of another man, with a gaff, which is a pole with an iron hook at the end, is needed, to bring it on board.[6]

The author of *The Perfect Storm*, the gripping story of the 1991 loss of a fishing vessel on the Grand Banks, says of the early fishermen of Gloucester (about a dozen miles up the coast from Marblehead),

> The shoulder muscles that resulted from a lifetime of such work made fishermen easily recognizable on the street. They were called 'hand-liners' and people got out of their way.[7]

A mature cod (3–6 years old) weighed 10–20 pounds (though inshore they were likely to be smaller), but their size varied and a 50-pound cod was not unusual. On Kimball's schooner *Mechanic* in 1825 (the figures are not available for the *Garland*), each man caught an average of 23 fish per day during the spring fare, 72 generally smaller fish per day during the summer fare, and 20 (full-size) fish per day during the fall fare. The average weight per live fish for the *Mechanic* in this year was 10–18 pounds during the spring fare, 4–8 pounds during the summer fare, and 12–23 pounds during the fall fare.[8]

At the end of each day's fishing, the men cleaned the fish, putting the livers into "the cod liver butt lashed alongside the rail just forward of the main rigging,

Model of Schooner Friendship. Early 1800s. By Captain John Bridgeo. Abbott Public Library

to dry out in the sun for the cod liver oil, a fine odorous compound after a month or so, but not unpleasant after one became accustomed to it, and very healthful."[9] Cod liver oil was used for curing leather, illumination, and medicine. The cod tongues and sounds (air bladders) were also saved by the men to eat at home. The fish were salted to preserve them at sea.[10] The position of salter "was only held by an experienced hand, as too free use of salt would waste it, while not enough would cause the fish to burn or turn red, something that would hurt its marketable value." Cooking was done in the fo'c'sle in a pot suspended over a fireplace built of brick under a scuttle, but "the forepeak was generally so filled with smoke that one could not see across it." This allowed the crew to smoke the "napes" of halibut for consumption at home.

Schooners rather than other rigs were used because of their ease of handling and because their fore-and-aft rigging enabled them to sail to windward against the prevailing southwest winds when coming back fully laden from the fishing banks.[11] A schooner had a large gaff-rigged mainsail aft, and a smaller gaff-rigged foresail and jib. The Marblehead Public Library has a fine model of an early-nineteenth-century fishing schooner, which clearly shows the common features of a schooner of this period: bluff bows; a long bowsprit; deck compartments to hold fish caught by the eight fishermen, and for cleaning fish; a conch horn and hourglass swinging from the fore boom; a large lantern hanging from the starboard main shrouds; a large raised quarterdeck; a tiller to steer with; a square stern; and striped topsides. This model was built in about 1865 by John Bridgeo, who began fishing with his father, Philip Bridgeo, as a boy of 13 in 1834, and later became captain of a clipper ship, as recounted below.[12]

After stacking the hold with 330 quintals (112 pounds per quintal) of salted cod, Snow headed the *Garland* for home, which they reached on June 4, after two and a half months on the Banks. The son of a Marblehead skipper describes the scene at home after a schooner returned as

> ...[q]uite a little jubilee. How delicately were the gradations of kinship and acquaintanceship expressed by the different gifts which the happy children were deputed to carry round! The outer circle received only "sea-crackers," that is, crackers left over from those carried, and impregnated by the briny flavor of the sea. The next circle inward received with the crackers a bit of smoked halibut; and those still more favored, in addition to the crackers and halibut, some "tongues and sounds." To all these luxuries, for the inner circle a halibut's fin was

added; and the crowning point of goodwill was a "hagdon"—a sea-bird of too rank a savor to be universally enjoyed.[13]

Meanwhile, the crew washed the salt off the fish in the harbor and laid them out in the open on platforms (called fences or flakes) for drying. As described by Samuel Roads, the principal historian of Marblehead,

> The fish fences … covered every available hill and headland on the mainland and a portion of the harbor side of the neck.… The work of curing or "making" fish, as it was called, required some skill and constant attention. After the fish had been spread out on the fences, it was necessary to turn them over from time to time in order to dry them to the necessary degree of hardness. This work was usually done by men hired for the purpose under the supervision of the owners. As some of the fish were intended for export to Bilbao or Jamaica, it was necessary to dry them very hard, it being a long voyage to one port, and the other being in a warm climate.… Vessels which had been on what was called the "spring fare" arrived home in the latter part of the month of May, and as their fish were not so heavily salted and were cured early in the season, they were considered of a better quality and brought a better price. The fall fish also brought a better price than those caught in the summer.[14]

When well cured, cod could be stored almost indefinitely.[15] Early in this period, the best fish were sold to Europe, primarily the Catholic countries of Spain, Portugal, and France, with trading voyages being made during the winter months, and the return trip from Europe bringing salt from the same countries.[16] Salt cod (bacalhao) is still a delicious staple in Portugal. The less good fish were sold to the West Indies for the slaves working on the sugar plantations, and the return voyage brought salt, or molasses and sugar from which rum was made. The French and Spanish West Indies were the most important foreign markets after the War of 1812. As time went on, more fish were sold within the United States.[17]

Cod (usually the Atlantic cod, *gadus morhua*) is nearly omnivorous, feeding both day and night on "any and every invertebrate small enough for it to swallow," as well as small fish. It favors rocky and pebbly ground, "except when following prey or on some journey," prefers water temperature of 35–50° F, and is found from 40 to 70 degrees North latitude in the western Atlantic.[18] It migrates to spawn (primarily in winter, which is why the bounty law, discussed in chapter 3, did not cover winter fishing), and seasonally, but "[f]ishermen have known from time immemorial that bodies of cod undertake extensive journeys with no apparent cause."[19] Besides man, its predators are seals and sharks. After four or more centuries of immense productivity, the codfishery has now collapsed because of overfishing.[20]

After a brief time at home, some of which was spent in preparing the *Garland* for its next fare, the same crew headed out again to the Grand Banks on June 23. Most fishing schooners did not have navigators capable of doing the laborious computations necessary to determine longitude with a chronometer and sextant for the voyage to the Grand Banks, or the occasional voyage to the Labrador coast. Instead, they used a compass, perhaps a quadrant to determine the altitude of sun or stars above the horizon in order to measure latitude, a lead line to determine the depth and the composition of the bottom, a rather rudimentary chart, experience, and luck.[21]

Originally, Marbleheaders had fished inshore grounds, and they began to fish George's Bank, to the east of Cape Cod, between 1720 and 1740. Then, following the fish, they moved farther offshore in larger vessels. By the period of this narrative, the Grand Banks, the shallow fishing region of the North Atlantic to the southeast of the island of Newfoundland, were the principal codfishing grounds of Marbleheaders.[22] Rising from the continental shelf, the Grand Banks cover some 139,000 square miles—almost the size of California and about 15 times the size of Massachusetts. Their depth varies from 100 to 600 feet, breaking the surface at the Virgin Rocks.

The Grand Banks had been fished for centuries from Europe:

> The Newfoundland fishery was commenced in the year 1504, by vessels from Biscay, Bretagne, and Normandy, in France. Its increase was rapid. In 1517, it employed as many as 50 vessels of different nations of Europe, and in 1577, the number was 350. The next year, Bancroft says, that "four hundred vessels came annually from the harbours of Portugal and Spain, of France and England." In the year 1593, Sir Walter Raleigh declared that this fishery was the stay of the west counties of England. In 1603, there were engaged in it 200 vessels, and, including the *shoresmen* or curers, 10,000 men. The fishermen then, as now, expended in the winter what they earned in the summer.[23]

The Grand Banks continued to be fished by large numbers of Europeans after 1815, particularly by the French.[24] The French migratory fishery left France in the spring and returned in the fall. In consideration of a generous Government bounty (see chapter 3), they were subject to being called to serve in the navy. By 1830, the French migratory fishing fleet "had grown to between 300 and 400 vessels manned by upward of 12,000 mariners."[25] The French often used a trawl line containing many hooks.[26]

The salient characteristic of the Grand Banks is fog, caused by the confluence of the Gulf Stream and the colder Labrador Current.

> A fisherman often spends weeks on the Banks without seeing a vessel, although hundreds are on the ground. This is owing partly to the fogs which abound there, and partly to the immense extent of that portion of the Atlantic known as the Grand Bank.[27]

Another writer describes a fare to the Grand Banks in 1861 from Marblehead in the *Rhody Carter*, skippered by Captain Clapp:

> A dense wall of fog shut out every object from view beyond a few yards. Here we lay for some hours nearly in a calm, occasionally tossing over a handful of bait to attract any shoals of fish that might be passing. There was no evidence of our being in the company of any other vessel, but as we listened someone heard the sound of blows close to windward. It was the cook of an invisible fisherman splitting wood for the galley. The skipper hailed at random:
> "Schooner ahoy!"
> "Hello!" answered a voice through the fog.
> "How's fishin"?"
> "Tolerable scuss. Who are yew?"
> "*Rhody Carter.* What schooner's that?"
> "*Mary Jane*, from Gloucester."....
> There was something strange, and almost mysterious, in thus being a whole day within speaking distance of persons whom we were unable to see. As night came on the fog became even more dense, so that we were unable to see five fathoms around the vessel. A continued drizzling rain dripped from the sails and rigging, while a solemn calm settled upon the ocean, attended with a long northeasterly swell. The appearance of the ocean during these calms in a high northern latitude is peculiarly sad, and it requires all the buoyancy of the sailor's temperament to resist its depressing influence. For days together the silence is unbroken but by the splash of some inhabitant of the watery world around us, or the cry of the sea-fowl that wing silently over the glassy waves.... Sometimes the continuous fog hanging along the ocean opens and reveals the shadowy outline of a vessel hull down on the horizon; or the increasing cold and the "blink" in the sky shows where the great currents from the polar seas are bearing southward the pinnacled icebergs, daily diminishing in size as they leave behind them the frigid regions of their birth.[28]

This writer describes the Marbleheaders much as Hawthorne's ancestor had:

A Marblehead fisherman is a splendid though rough specimen of an American. You may know him by his free-and-easy manner and swinging gait.... His face is a reflex of a rather serious but cheerful and contented spirit; the result of a philosophical, half careless dependence upon luck. He is generous and fearless in his address, of simple and economical habits, and like most men of large stature, almost peculiar in a placid good-humor which rarely leaves him. Always ready for any fortune, the fisherman endeavors to look upon the brightest side of life, and expect whatever there may be of pleasure in his hazardous calling. But among them are occasional roistering, devil-may-care fellows, whose never-ending practical jokes and off-hand manner serve to enliven the little vessel and dispel the monotony of the voyage.

As Justice Joseph Story would later say of seamen generally, "They partake ... somewhat of the boisterousness of the element which they navigate."

An evocative description of fishing in the fog is found in *An Iceland Fisherman* (1886) by Pierre Loti, himself a seaman, about a French cod fisherman in Iceland waters:

They stayed there this time ten days together, caught in the thick fog, and seeing nothing. The fishing continued good, and they were too busy to talk. From time to time, at regular intervals, one of them blew on a fog horn, which gave out a sound like the bellow of a wild beast.

And sometimes, from far in the depth of the white mist, another bellowing like it would answer to their call. And then the man on the lookout was more watchful than ever; and if the sound came nearer, all ears listened for the unknown neighbor, whom they would probably never be able to see, but whose proximity was nevertheless a danger.

And they would make conjectures as to what ship it could be, and that made an occupation for them; it seemed a sort of company for them, and they tried hard in their eagerness to see something, to look through the impalpable white muslin curtains which hung everywhere about them in the air.

Then the sound would retreat, and the bellowings of the trumpet die away and be lost in the dull distance; and they would find themselves alone again in the deep stillness, in the midst of the infinite motionless mist. Everything became impregnated with water and dripped with salt and brine. The cold became more penetrating; the sun hung still lower over the horizon; and they began to have two or three hours of real night, which closed in over them in a gray and somber chill....

Their life, though rough, was a healthy one; and the biting cold made their evenings seem more comfortable, and heightened the pleasant feeling of warmth and shelter which they found on going down into their massive oak cabin to sleep or eat.

During the day, these men, who were more isolated than cloistered monks, talked little to one another. They would stay hours and hours at the same post, each holding his line, their arms alone occupied in the constant work of fishing. Though only separated by two or three yards, they finished by taking no notice of one another.

The calm of the fog and its white obscurity had dulled their brains. While fishing, they would sing some old ballad, but softly, under their breath, for fear of frightening away the fish.

Their thoughts came very slowly, and there were fewer of them, seeming to expand and stretch themselves out, in order to fill up the time without leaving any gaps or intervals of blankness in the mind.

And sometimes their thoughts wandered off into incoherent and marvelous dreams, as if in sleep; and the woof of these dreams was as vague and floating as a vapor.[29]

The Grand Banks are located on the busy route of ships sailing or steaming from New York or Boston to Europe and back, and the prevalence of fog created a serious risk of collision with one of the hundreds of fishing vessels on the banks, despite the size of the area. There are stories of such collisions by Washington Irving, where no survivors are found, and by Herman Melville, with minimal damage, and others describe near misses.[30] The newspaper column "Disasters &c.," selected at random, also reports "contact" on the fishing banks.

Fishing sch *Beverly*, of Beverly, having 16,000 fish on board, was run into on Grand Bank, by a British ship, which lay by her all night, and on leaving gave up her long boat for the use of the crew, if it should be found necessary. The Beverly has been spoken by a Cape Cod fisherman, working slowly homeward.[31]

Capt Brown, of the Brig *Keying*, arrived at Boston, reports— ... Sept 10 8:30 PM, wind heavy from NE; came in contact with fishing sch *Empire*, of New London, then lying to. The sch immediately fell alongside, and all her crew (6 in number) got on board the brig. The sea running too high to risk further communication, we filled away, all safe on board the *K*, and uncertain what damage the sch had sustained. Left her, Georges [Bank] (NE part) bearing SE 7 or 8 leagues. If the sch had a light on deck, no doubt the accident would have been avoided. Capt B felt compelled to make the best of his way to this port, as he was almost entirely out of provisions.[32]

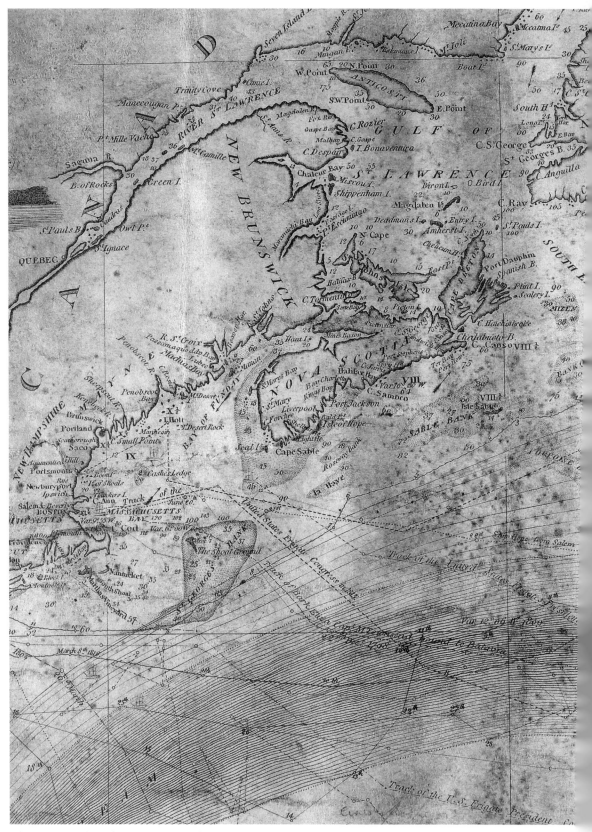

Chart of Grand Banks (From 1826 Blunt). Courtesy of the Peabody Essex Museum, Salem, Mass.

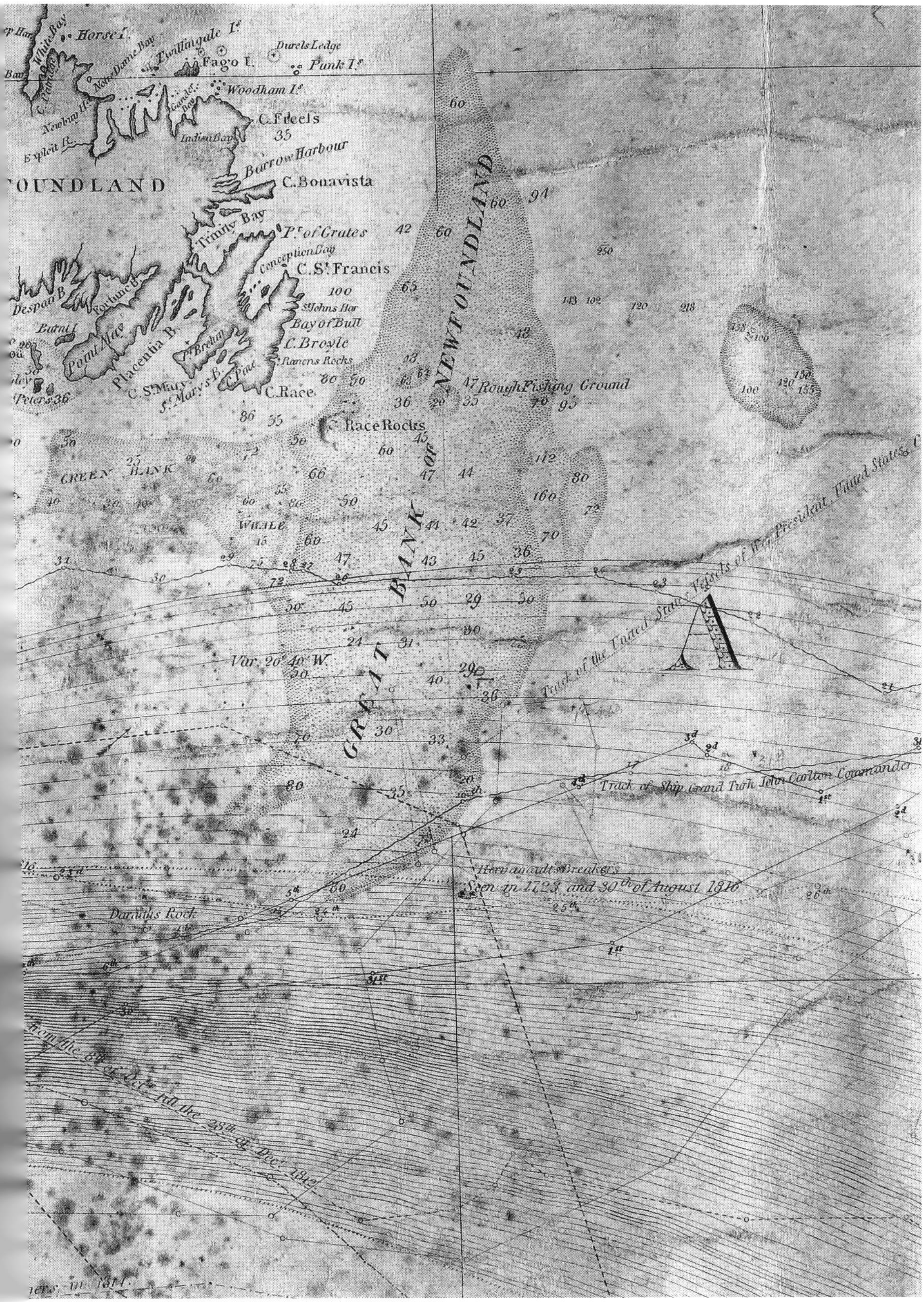

OUNDLAND

Horse I. Twillingate Is.
Fago I. Durels Ledge
Punk I.
Woodham Is.
C. Freels 35
Barrow Harbour
C. Bonavista
P.t of Grates 42 60
Trinity Bay
Conception Bay 65
C. St Francis 100
St Johns Har
Bay of Bull
C. Broyle
Ravens Rocks
C. St Mary's 80 50
C. Pine
St Marys B. C. Race 36 50
Despoo B.
Burnt I.
Point May
Placentia B.
Fortune B.
Peters 36 86 35

NEWFOUNDLAND

60
60 94
60
850
143 192 120 218
215
100
150
120 155
42
47 Rough Fishing Ground
43 78 93
20 35
36 112
45 80
60 47 44 160 72
70
GREEN BANK 25 66
WHALE 45 41 42 37
60 15
31 72 43 15 36
8 47
50 45 50 29 50
24 31 80
Var. 20° 40' W. 90
50 40 29
36
30 33
60 35
24
Darulis Rock

GREAT BANK

Track of the United States Vessels of War President. United States C.
A
Track of the United States
Track of Ship Grand Turk John Carlton Commander
3d 2d
18
1st
2d
1st

Hernanault's Breakers
Seen in 1723 and 30th of August 1810
25th
1st
3rd

Race Rocks

In a rare lawsuit in 1870, a fishing schooner sued a sailing ship that struck it when anchored on the Grand Banks in the fog, killing 9 of her 10 crew. "The fog had been prevailing for four or five days, and was so thick that nothing could be seen more than half the length of the ship ahead." The ship was going about six knots, carrying all canvas except studding sails, maintaining a lookout, and sounding a fog horn. When the fishermen heard the ship, they hastily sounded a horn, rather than a bell as required by a Federal statute enacted in 1864. The court found that the schooner was at fault in this, and that the speed of the ship did not contribute to the collision, and therefore decided that the schooner could not recover damages.[33]

> One of [the witnesses for the ship, as to the duty of masters of vessels sailing in a fog] stated that he never shortened sail, in all his experience, in a fog, his view being, that the faster a ship goes, the quicker she will answer her helm, and, therefore, the less the danger of colliding with another vessel. Another witness stated, that the proper course, in a fog, is, not to shorten sail at all, but to go as fast as you can, and take the chances, using every prudent precaution. Another stated, that he never made less sail on account of a fog, and that the rule is to go as fast as you can, consistently with wind and weather. Another stated, that it is as prudent to go as fast as you can, through a fog, as long as the masts hold in. Another stated, that he never diminishes his speed in a fog on the Banks, his object being to get through the fog as quickly as possible, lest he should be run into. Another stated, that he always crosses the Banks in a fog as fast as he can, and that it is not more dangerous to a vessel, at anchor there, in a fog, for another vessel to go fast than to go at less speed....
>
> Two prominent ideas were advanced by the witnesses for the [ship] in this case, as justifying undiminished speed in a fog on the Banks. One was, that the danger to any vessel in a fog is greater the longer she remains in a fog. The other was, that the faster a vessel is going the more quickly she will mind her helm, and thus the better she will be able, on a signal of danger, to avoid colliding with another vessel, in a fog. Neither of these ideas has any sanction in the law, and any vessel which acts upon them takes upon herself the consequences of recklessness. The first idea disregards wholly the rights and the safety of other vessels. The other idea presupposes that a signal of danger, proceeding from a vessel unseen in a fog, to another vessel, will necessarily be heard so seasonably, and acted upon so intelligently, by the latter, as to secure, by a proper movement of her helm, the avoidance of a collision.

Nevertheless, the court was unable to find that, in this case, the collision was owing to the speed of the ship being too great.

As noted in *The Perfect Storm*, the Grand Banks also sit on one of the worst storm tracks in the world.[34] Death at sea was an ever-present risk for fishermen, as well as other mariners.[35] As Lucy Larcom (1824–93), an author and poet from Beverly, says:

> The pathos of the sea haunted the town, made audible to every ear when a coming northeaster brought the rote of the waves in from the islands across the harbor-bar, with a moaning like that we heard when we listened for it in the shell. Almost every house had its sea-tragedy. Somebody belonging to it had been shipwrecked, or had sailed away one day, and never returned.[36]

Her poem "Hannah Binding Shoes" ends:

> Twenty winters
> Bleach and tear the ragged shore she views.
> Twenty seasons:-
> Never one has brought her any news.
> Still her dim eyes silently
> Chase the white sails o'er the sea:
> Hopeless, faithful,
> Hannah's at the window, binding shoes.

Marblehead had many widows and orphans, but widows sometimes married again, and orphans sometimes were adopted by other family members. Like farming families of the time, fishing families were large by today's standards, but often women did not survive the rigors of bearing large numbers of children, and a widower sometimes married again before accumulating a dozen children. Several societies were organized in Marblehead to assist those engaged in the fishery, including the Marblehead Marine Society (1798), the Social Fisheries Club (1805), the Marblehead Female Humane Society (1816), and the Marblehead Charitable Seaman's Society (1831).[37]

The *Garland* returned to Marblehead on September 27, 1825, with 580 quintals of cod, making its catch for the year a total of 910 quintals. The date was earlier than the usual return of the schooners in November, and the *Garland*'s catch was less than the *Mechanic*'s 980 quintals, the *Hope*'s 1,400 quintals, and the 1,000 quintals generally considered to be a good year's catch.[38]

ENDNOTES

1   The crew took turns cooking to save money, Roads p. 366. Boys were like apprentice fishermen.

2   He married Elizabeth Bowden in 1811, but she died in 1820 of consumption (Snow Genealogy, Corinne A. and Frank B. Snow, 1979). The birth dates of several of the children are not given. Samuel Snow's brother John Picket Snow died in 1821, "Capt of Schooner *Cherub* at Point Peter, Guadaloup." Another brother, Thomas Snow, was also a skipper.

3   Whidden (1908) pp. 116–20. Whidden recounts how, out of curiosity, he undertook a fall fishing voyage in 1853 as navigator on the schooner *Ceres*, Skipper Joshua Nickerson.

4   Roads p. 365.

5   Wells pp. 467–68. The deposition of Jeremiah Roundy in the case of *Rich v. The Cherub*, 20 F. Cas. 668 (U.S.D.C.D. MA, 1823), at the National Archives and Records Administration, Waltham, MA (NARA), states that the Marblehead schooner *Cherub* purchased bread at Souris Harbor "on the Labrador shore," and picked up men who worked their passage to Marblehead. Souris Harbor, a large fishing and shipbuilding port in northeastern Prince Edward Island in the Gulf of St. Lawrence, also apparently was the place referred to by Circuit Justice Joseph Story (he called it "Cyrus Harbor, on the Labrador shore") as the "place vessels employed in the fisheries usually resort in the course of their voyages." *The Three Brothers*, 23 F. Cas. 1162 (Cir. Ct. MA, 1812). The coasts of the Gulf of St. Lawrence were often referred to as the "Labrador shore" by fishermen, according to Ralph Getson at the Fisheries Museum of the Atlantic in Lunenburg, Nova Scotia.

6   Reynolds (1856), a story about a fisherman from Pigeon Cove, Rockport, north of Marblehead. The first house in the area of Pigeon Cove was built by weaver Samuel Gott in 1702 near Halibut Point, and is still standing. Wells, p. 459.

7   Junger (1998), "Gloucester, Mass., 1991," p. 26.

8   "On the average, 288 pounds of round cod (fish as caught, not dressed) produced 193 pounds of split cod and 112 pounds [1 quintal] of dried fish suitable for New England markets. A quintal of the driest export fish required 350 pounds of split cod" (German, 1987, pp. 419). This is a dry-to live-weight ratio of 1:2.6. Another source gives a conversion ratio for cod of 1:4.9 (ISER Conf. Pap. No. 5, 1995, Peter Pope at n. 7, p. 36). It is impossible to be more precise without knowing the dryness of the fish sold. Wells gives the average weight of fish during his voyage in 1861 as 14 pounds, p. 459.

9   Whidden p. 118.

10 Salt draws water out of bacteria and fungal cells, inhibiting their growth. The drying process was begun by stacking the cleaned and salted fish in the hold, which forced out some of the moisture.

11 Chapelle (1973) p. 37.

12 The plaque on the model reads: "Marblehead Fishing Schooner *Friendship* Representing an Early 19th Century Vessel, $^3/_8$" Scale Model Built by Capt John Bridgeo *c.* 1865. Exhibited at Centennial Exposition in Philadelphia in 1876 and at the Smithsonian Institution." The size of the model indicates that the schooner was about 64 feet in length, a typical size. Several schooners named *Friendship* were involved in fishing and foreign trade from Marblehead in the early 19th century (Bradlee). The Cape Ann Historical Museum in Gloucester also has two models of fishing schooners from 1820 (*Manchester*) and 1836 (*Congress*), both built about 1870.

13 Chadwick (1874) p. 195.

14 Roads pp. 353–55.

15 Ryan (1986) p. 29.

16 McFarland pp. 95–97, 141–42. Fish were sometimes sold by the fishermen in Nova Scotia or Labrador and shipped directly to Europe (Edmund Kimball's account book p. 41, hereafter Account Book); McFarland p. 154.

17 Ryan pp. 84, 101, 226–27, 230, 234. Hutchins (1941) pp. 252–53. Tariffs in the British West Indies favored British colonies, such as Newfoundland. By 1840, three quarters of the New England catch was consumed inside the United States (Vickers, 1994, pp. 275–76). Bentley says in April 1818: "Marblehead rising from the success of the fishery. They have a vent for fish in the interior & through Albany last year great quantities have passed into the western counties." Bentley, vol. IV, p. 514.

18 Food and Agriculture Organization, United Nations, www.fao.org.

19 Bigelow and Welsh (1925) pp. 409–422.

20 A 1992 historical review revealed "that the Georges Bank cod stock seemed resilient to heavy fishing pressure until the early- and mid-1980s when landings, fishing effort and fishing mortality approached or attained record-high levels" (Serchuk and Wigley, 1992). In 2002, the Northeast Fisheries Science Center of the National Oceanic and Atmospheric Administration concluded: "In 1995, landings [of Georges Bank cod] reached a record low … and have remained relatively constant since that time…. Although strict management regulations implemented in 1994 reduced the fishing mortality on Georges Bank cod for both the U.S. and Canada, the stock does not appear to be responding positively" (Northeast Fisheries Science Center, 2002). There is evidence that overfishing began to affect cod stocks in the early to mid-1800s

(Hutchings, 1995). The reasons for this calamity are another story. Today scientists are attempting to learn, through tagging of individual fish and studying the contents of their stomachs, what some Marbleheaders may have known in a less scientific way, but did not record, about the behavior of the cod (Nielsen and Andersen, 2001).

21   Wells p. 471. Charts of the northeast coast of the United States prior to 1821 showed Nantucket South Shoal 22 miles out of position, and described Georges Bank "imperfectly." *Blunt v. Patten*, 3 F. Cas. 763 (Cir. Ct. N. Y., 1828) (a successful case of copyright infringement brought by the author of an 1821 chart that corrected these errors against another person who had copied his chart). Fortunately from the point of view of safety, these charts showed Nantucket South Shoal extending *too* far south, rather than not far enough—though of course, the position of shoals constantly shifts. Fishermen may also have used a log line and a half-minute glass to determine speed and distance. In Kipling's *Captains Courageous* (1896), Gloucester fishermen were depicted as still using a quadrant (rather than the more modern sextant) of a type called a hog-yoke. "...[H]e took the sun, and with the help of 'The Old Farmers' almanac found the latitude.... The said 'hog-yoke,' an Eldridge chart, the farming almanac, Blunt's 'Coast Pilot,' and Bowditch's 'Navigator' were all the weapons Disko [skipper of the *We're Here*] needed to guide him, except the deep-sea lead that was his spare eye" (chapter 5).

22   "Unaccountably, there is no evidence that Marbleheaders returned to George's Bank after the [Revolutionary] war, and they never frequented George's Bank again" (German pp. 409–11).

23   Senator John Davis of Massachusetts (1787–1854) in a speech to the Senate, quoted in *North American Review* 120 (1843): 78–81. See also Janzen.

24   After 1815, "[s]hips engaging in the banks fishery left France in the early spring for St.-Pierre, where they took on provisions, especially of bait, and went to fish on the Grand Banks" (Wilkshire, 1998).

25   Baehre (1999) p. 176. The French could dry their fish on the "French shore," the west coast and northern peninsula of Newfoundland. A letter written by a British "colonist" and published in 1860 states: "France has now in the fisheries of Newfoundland alone more than twenty thousand sailors employed. These men are all subject to naval discipline, they go out in the spring, and return to France in the autumn; they are at all times liable to be called out to serve in the navy....These men and boys are taught seamanship in a rugged school; they are inured to hardships, seasoned to cold, to storms, and the roughest work of the seaman....In 1841, when war with England was apprehended, M. Thiers recalled the fishermen, absent in Newfoundland, to enter the navy." "The Manning of the French Navies, and the North American Fisheries Question," 66 *The Living Age* 846, August 16, 1860.

26   Cadigan (1995), p. 344.

27 Reynolds p. 58.

28 Wells pp. 457–61.

29 Loti (1890) pp. 152–154. Pierre Loti (1850–1923) was born Louis Marie Julien Viaud in Rochefort, near L'Isle d'Oleron on the west coast of France. He became a naval officer, and was elected to the French Academy for his writings. The French ocean codfishing fleet, based in Paimpol, Brittany, changed its fishing grounds from Newfoundland to Iceland during the late 19th century (Magnusson, 1993).

30 "The Voyage" in Irving (1835); chapter 19 in Melville (1849); Chadwick (1906) p. 72; Roads, p. 370.

31 *Boston Shipping List*, August 8, 1846.

32 *Boston Shipping List*, September 16, 1846.

33 *The Chancellor*, 5 F. Cas. 439 (D.C.N.Y., 1870). The suit was brought to recover for the damage to the schooner and her fish; there was no right to recover for the wrongful death of the fishermen. Wells pp. 469–470.

34 Junger, "God's Country," p. 55.

35 Baehre contains contemporaneous accounts of shipwrecks in Newfoundland waters, including the loss of two French fishing vessels in 1826, one with the loss of 106 crew-members. Kimball's vessels were no exception. Robert Atkins, Jr. died "at sea in the Schooner *America*, Benj Graves, Master" in 1822. The Marblehead Marine Insurance Company records for 1832 show a total loss on a policy for $400 issued to John and Abiel Roads on the first of Edmund Kimball's schooners named *Mary*; the loss took place on a voyage from Marblehead to Bay Chaleur (south of Gaspé) (Phillips Library, Peabody Essex Museum, Salem, Ms. 140, book 32, #4701). Alexander McIntosh "drowned in the Harbour from Sch *William*" in 1836 at 32 years of age. Joseph Bessom died "at sea, Drowned from Barque *Mary Kimball*" (VRM). And there were many others. In *Captains Courageous*, Kipling describes the annual memorial service for fishermen in Gloucester, and the Wall of Remembrance added in 2000 to Leonard Craske's 1923 Fishermen's Memorial there names the 5,379 Gloucester fishermen who had died at sea since 1716. Today, "more people are killed in fishing boats, per capita, than in any other job in the United States." Junger, "The Flemish Cap," p.88.

36 Larcom (1889), chapter 5.

37 Tutt. The history of the Marblehead Female Humane Society, run entirely by women, was written by Martha Bessom Gorman in 1987, when it was still in operation. The Social Fishery Club listed 103 members in 1805. Marblehead Museum and Historical Society.

38. Roads, p. 335.

THREE

Codfishing as a Livelihood: Samuel Snow

Samuel Snow continued as skipper of the *Garland* in 1826 and 1827, and in 1828, after the *Garland* was sold, he took over as skipper of the 55-foot schooner *Eliza*. The skipper was responsible for putting together a crew for the voyage, as capable and congenial as possible. Snow began the task by bringing Joseph Severy (25) and George Melzard with him from the *Garland*, and then added Benjamin Severy (27) and Peter Severy (17), brothers of Joseph, and Jacob Maine. The *Eliza* made three fares in 1828, for a total catch of about 1,061 quintals—a good year. The fish were sold to various buyers for prices ranging from $3.13 per quintal for the spring fare to $2.15 for the fall fare, making an average of about $2.58 per quintal—a moderate rate.

The owner of the vessel was deemed to own the fish that had been caught, and under the standard agreement between the owner, skipper, and crew, the owner was required to render to the crew a true account of the sale of the fish. From the proceeds of the sale would be deducted the cost of the general supplies provided by the owner (the "great generals," such as bait and salt), and also the traditional share of the owner in the remaining balance, which was 3/8 in Marblehead.[1] Lesser and greater shares—ranging from 1/5 to 3/4—were taken by owners in other ports.[2] The 3/8 was the same as the proportion of the bounty allowed to the owner by statute, and theoretically represented the shoreman's compensation for curing the fish (1/8) plus the owner's compensation for use of the vessel (1/4).[3] The remaining 5/8 was apportioned among the skipper and crew in proportion to the number of fish caught by each, or by pre-determined shares, and then each man's share of the "small generals" (supplies for the crew, principally food) was deducted from his portion.[4] The custom in Marblehead was for the fishermen to be paid only when the owner had actually sold the fish and received payment from the buyer. For fares that extended into the fall, the sale of fish often did not occur until the following spring. Like a farmer before his crop is harvested and sold, therefore, the fishermen would need credit for purchases unrelated to the fishing voyage.[5] Behind this accounting are hundreds of years of tradition in the Marblehead codfishery.

In addition, the participants were entitled to a share of a special subsidy from the Federal government, known as a bounty. The Federal bounty to vessels in the codfishery was first passed in 1789, in only the second act of the new Federal Congress, and by the late 1820s amounted to $4 per ton (for vessels over 30 tons) per year.[6] As stated by the U.S. Supreme Court:

> The inducement to the payment of these bounties was, the public policy of training a body of native seamen, by an industrious pursuit of the cod fishery during a fixed portion of the year. To accomplish this, it was deemed important that the seamen should participate directly in the profits of the voyage.[7]

The French had had a bounty for fishermen since as early as 1762 for the same reason—as a "nursery for their seamen."

> The policy of the French, from their first planting colonies in America, insists particularly on raising seamen for their navy by means of the fisheries. The nature of the French fishery was always such, that one-third, or at least one-fourth, of the men employed in it were 'green men,' or men who were never before at sea; and by this trade they bred up from 4,000 to 6,000 seamen annually.[8]

The year 1828 is the first for which Edmund Kimball's account book contains detailed records of his various schooners.[9] The account for the schooner *Eliza*'s spring 1828 voyage can be summarized as follows:[10]

Accounting for Schooner Eliza's Spring fare 1828

proceeds of fish	$1,116
deduct great generals	309
balance	806
deduct owner's 3/8ths	302
balance	504

The major items in the great generals were 51 hogsheads (63 gallons per hogshead) of salt, $219; 6 barrels of mackerel (bait), $36; and "barrow carrying," $10. Salt, which included a stiff import duty, was a very costly item, about 20 percent of the proceeds of the voyage.[9] The balance of the proceeds after these deductions was shared among the crew as follows:

Samuel Snow caught	1,687 fish	$86	
Joseph Severy	1,687	86	
George Melzard	1,687	86	(signed by an X)
Jacob Maine	1,687	86	
Benjamin Severy	1,687	86	
Peter Severy	1,386	71	
total	9,821	504	

From each fisherman's share was deducted one sixth of the small generals, which was $10, so five of the crew would earn $76 for this fare, and the boy (Peter Severy) $61. The largest expenses in the small generals were 2¾ cords wood, $16 (it was cold out there), and beef, $9. Snow's crews were frugal, foregoing the services of a cook and eating mostly fish they caught; the crew took turns cooking, employing a variety of culinary styles with the same ingredients. Various other expenses are occasionally charged to the crew, such as rum and gin, hooks and line (sometimes identified as mackerel hooks for bait; generally, the crew fished for cod "on their own hook"), "making" (curing) of fish, hats and shoes, and cartage and wharfage.[12] Also included in both the great and small generals is an additional amount of 10 percent for the owner ($28 for the great generals and $5 for the small). In one instance in Kimball's account book this is broken down in the great generals as 8 percent advance (that is, interest on the generals supplied) and 2 percent insurance, but the 10 percent is never omitted.[13] When the 10 percent is added to the owner's share of this voyage, the total is $335. These accounting conventions heavily favored the owner by eliminating almost all his risk.[14]

To a fisherman's share of $76 was added his share of the other two fares for that year ($29 and $46), and, at the end of the year, his share of the Federal bounty ($4 times 55 tons = $219), or about $22, for a total of $173 for the year 1828. This was not a bad year, and the *Eliza*'s earnings were the best of any of Kimball's

schooners that year: fishermen on the *Sally* (62 feet, four men and four boys, skippered by Philip Bridgeo, two fares) made $151.87; on the *Ploughboy* (63 feet, six
men and two boys, skippered by William Hammond, two fares), $166.56; on the
Hope (61 feet, five men and three boys, skippered by John White, two fares), $142;
on the *Mechanic* (55 feet, six men and one boy, skippered by Joseph Tucker, two
fares), $61; and on the *Lewis* (48 feet, nine men and two boys, skippered by Samuel
Green, one fare to Labrador) only $33. The *Mechanic* and the *Lewis* had very poor
catches, and their skippers were not employed by Kimball again. Voyages to Labrador, like that of the *Lewis*, left later in the spring, were longer and more dangerous, had a shorter fishing season, used larger crews, and were thus less profitable
than voyages to the banks.[15] The Labrador fishery was an experiment that didn't
pan out. Marblehead schooners did not go there often in later years.

Then, as now, fishing was not a predictable means of earning a living; there
was large variation in a fisherman's annual earnings.[16] But, as Story said, Marbleheaders had "an indifference to the show and splendor of wealth, which cannot be
easily imagined." A Marblehead fisherman worked an average of eight months of
the year at fishing and related activities, and he could work at other occupations the
rest of the time if he wanted to.[17]

To qualify for the Federal bounty, the law required: that the proceeds of the
voyage be divided among the fishermen (excluding the cook) in proportion to the
number of fish caught; that 3/4 of the crew be U.S. citizens; that no more than 3/8
of the bounty be paid to the owner; and that the vessel have been at sea in the codfishery for four months.[18] When the Marblehead schooner *Mary and Hannah* was
lost with all her crew in 1834, a special Act of Congress provided for the payment
of her bounty.[19] The average bounty per fisherman was about $25, roughly 10-20%
of a fisherman's earnings.[20] Vessels were also required by law to be enrolled in
coastal trade or registered in foreign trade, as well as licensed in the codfishery.

As the years passed, the bounty was opposed by some as a subsidy or protection
for the codfishery. In 1839, to defend fishermen against critics who said they were
"ignorant, superstitious, and improvident," Massachusetts Senator John Davis
made a long speech in the U.S. Senate, with many historical allusions, some of
which are obscure to a modern ear:

> The thirty pieces of silver bought their man—but not among those
> who had cast their nets in the sea of Galilee. The battle of Worcester
> was lost to the second Charles, and he fled for his life; and who were
> more true to him, in his hour of need, than the fishermen?... And to
> look into our own history, was no disquiet entertained, when Phips

attained to the chief magistracy, under William and Mary's new charter to Massachusetts? Why, even the Indians of Maine, says a historian, were "amazed" at the elevation to such dignity, of one with whom they "had hunted and fished for many a weary day"… A fisherman of Maine captured more guns during our Revolutionary war than any other naval commander in the service; but how many knew so much of him as his name [Samuel Tucker]?… But the labors and sufferings of those who, throughout [the first century of our history], constantly visited our seas in search of fish, ought not thus to be disposed of. They were the pioneers of civilization.… The annual arrival on the coast of from one hundred to three and even four hundred vessels could not have failed to be the germ of some important events.…[21]

The bounty law remained on the books until 1866, and gave rise to a variety of litigation.[22] In the case of the *Harriet*, Circuit Justice Joseph Story had to determine whether the vessel was employed in the cod fishery, because it had taken hake.[23] He stated:

> We all know, that it is a common usage and incident to the cod fisheries, to fish for and to catch pollock, halibut, haddock, and other fish; and it has never been imagined, that this was not within the scope of the license. Until the mackerel fishery was, by the act of congress, separated into a distinct employment, it was frequently carried on in connection with, and as an incident to the cod fisheries. No one can now doubt, that mackerel may still be caught in the cod fisheries, if it be not so pursued, as to supersede the principal employment, but is a mere accessory or incidental fishery.

Story's knowledge of the codfishery from his early days in Marblehead clearly helped him in reaching this decision, as his general knowledge of maritime affairs assisted him in establishing many other aspects of maritime law.

The market price of fish fluctuated greatly during the years 1823–33, from a low of $1.88 to a high of $3.50 per quintal.[24] The years 1825–26 and 1829–30 were at the low end of the scale. During 1825–26, the catches on Kimball's schooners were about 1,000 quintals per year, but in 1827 and 1835, when the market price was at the high end of the scale, the catches were only about 700 quintals. This appears to be explicable by principles of supply and demand, though demand must have decreased with a near doubling of the price. To the extent that market prices rose as catches decreased, fishermen and owners did not benefit from the higher prices, having to work just as hard to catch 700 quintals and earn the same amount of money.

Skippers were required to keep a log, but no Marblehead logs have been found for this period, and fishermen, when they did write of their experiences, tended to say "no tongue can describe...."[25] An example of the ups and downs of a fisherman's life can be found in the story of skipper John W. Chadwick of Marblehead, as written by his son.[26] Born in 1809 to a fishing family, he began fishing at age 13 with an uncle, and made his first voyage to the Grand Banks in another schooner in March, 1824.

> It was a hard beginning. The first night it blew a heavy gale, so that a two-reef foresail was all the vessel could bear. It was bitter cold, and the smoke blew back into the forecastle, so that they could have no fire. In those days the fire was made in the companion-way. Seasick and homesick, the poor boy lay in his berth—a contracted one in the forepeak, the cook's usual place—nibbling a loaf of bread his mother had made for him, and salting it with tears. The next morning there were two feet of ice on deck.[27]

For the next six years (1825–30), he sailed with another uncle, skipper John White, in Edmund Kimball's *Hope*, "two fares each year, making at the best $200 a year."[28] In 1832, at age 22, he became the skipper of the *Ploughboy*, then owned by Josiah P. Creesy.

> Drink was one of the dangers with which he had to contend, his own temperance being always strict without being total abstinence. Once a drunken hand grew mutinous, but was brought to terms when the young skipper took up a windlass-bar, and with a strong expression threatened to knock out his brains.[29]

Chadwick suffered throughout his life from injuries incurred while fishing. In 1834 he married and bought a 1/3-share in a schooner. Beginning in 1825 he had made shoes during the winter, adding $50 to his annual earnings. On his fall fare in 1835, the vessel only caught 5.40 quintals. The next year he transferred his 1/3 ownership to a larger schooner, the *Hero* (86 tons), in which he fished through 1846.

In 1838 he cleared $700, in 1839 $400, and in 1840 he lost $50 on his first fare and barely made it up on the second. In 1842, when fish brought only $1.75 a quintal, he earned $250, and in 1843, $500. After the hurricane of 1846, which he survived in the *Hero*, but in which some of his relatives perished, he thought of quitting, but continued until 1859, at age 50, working thereafter as a shoemaker.[30]

Fishermen could supplement their income in other occupations when not fishing. In addition to shoemaking, which became common in Marblehead during this period, these included curing fish and crewing on voyages to Europe or the Caribbean.[31] Reynolds writes:

> A voyage to Europe, to the West Indies, or to the coast of South America, is, on the whole, the best employment for the fisherman in the winter. The great evil in the life of the fisherman is, that he is idle through the winter, and eats up, during that portion of the year, what he had earned in the summer. This it is that keeps most of them poor all their lives....
>
> Most of the men who go to the Banks in the summer, refuse altogether to engage in fishing in the winter, especially if they have had tolerable luck in the summer.[32]

Although fishermen's earnings seem low and fluctuated greatly, they gave the fisherman in six months more than a merchant seaman earned in a year at the then-current rate of $12 per month.[33] Morison observes:

> [E]x-fishermen were seldom found among the crews of deep-sea merchantmen, at any period of our history. "They make troublesome merchantmen," writes [Salem minister] Bentley of the Marblehead fishermen in 1816.

Morison attributes this to fishermen not being used to discipline, but it probably had more to do with their preferring the generally better earnings (given the time invested), the more egalitarian environment, and the time off available to a fisherman.[34] Why would a fisherman ever submit himself to a potentially abusive mate or captain for inferior earnings as a seaman on a merchant vessel? Few in Marblehead did, except those who as young men aimed to become captains in the merchant marine.

A merchant vessel had a severe hierarchical structure, in contrast to the egalitarian, communal structure of a fishing vessel.[35] Herman Melville describes the characteristics of merchant seamen from his own experience:

> Consider that, with the majority of them, the very fact of their being sailors, argues a certain recklessness and sensualism of character, ignorance, and depravity; consider that they are generally friendless and alone in the world; or if they have friends and relatives, they are almost constantly beyond the reach of their good influences; consider that after the rigorous discipline, hardships, dangers, and privations of a voyage, they are set adrift in a foreign port, and exposed to a thousand enticements, which, under the circumstances, would be hard even for virtue itself to withstand, unless virtue went about on crutches; consider that by their very vocation they are shunned by the better classes of people, and cut off from all access to respectable and improving society; consider

Front Street, Marblehead, near the wharfs, circa 1890. Courtesy of Historic New England/ SPNEA.

all this, and the reflecting mind must very soon perceive that the case of sailors, as a class, is not a very promising one.[36]

The distinction between friendless seamen adrift in a foreign port, and fishermen "whose voyages began and ended in the same port" was particularly striking in the close-knit community of Marblehead. Marblehead is a peninsular (almost insular) town, and many Marbleheaders were related to each other, sometimes in multiple ways. As recent inhabitant and author Russell Knight (a descendant of fishermen and schooner owners) put it:

> There was no real wealth running the show [in Marblehead]. Oh, there was a handful of rich folks—the Hoopers and the Lees—but they didn't get in anyone's way. This was *not* an oligarchy or anything like that. The secret was that the people were all of one ilk. They sailed with each other, only did business with each other, and married each other.[37]

Although each schooner had a skipper, who acted as captain and was the owner's representative on board, in Marblehead the skipper traditionally was not paid wages in addition to his share.[38] The only exception for Kimball's skippers was on the voyages to Labrador, and toward the end of his career when the skipper (usually on a single fare per year) received an additional 1/64 share, while Kimball took a 1/4 share (instead of the usual 3/8), and a shoreman a 1/14 or 1/15 share (instead of the usual 1/8).[39] There must have been other benefits to becoming a skipper, such as greater control over the voyage and prestige, that were sufficient to encourage skippers to take on the greater responsibility. Writers point out the means by which prestige was conferred upon a skipper:

> In the early days of the industry, it was a common custom for the skipper, after arrival in port and the anchorage and all things about the "banker" had been made secure, to don his tall hat, then called a "beaver" hat, come ashore and march up the wharf through lines of fellow citizens, who welcomed him home, as he passed by them on his way to his own home and family—thus adding a touch of dignity to the happy occasion.[40]

This practice contrasts with the incentive pay commonly given to masters of merchant vessels, but not to the crew, and the much closer association of masters of such vessels with the interests of the owner, as contrasted with those of the crew. The earnings incentive to catch more fish applied equally to all the crew (except the cook). This might be explained by the greater importance on fishing voyages of individual effort and skill, as contrasted with the teamwork character of crewing a larger vessel.[41] Whaling ships also used a share system for the whole crew, but with great differences in the amount of the shares among the various crewmembers.

Skippers who were successful in their schooner voyages for Kimball could rely on continued employment by him for many years; skippers who did not work out, usually because of low earnings, lasted only one year. Samuel Snow was skipper successively of the *Garland* (1825–27), the *Eliza* (1828), and the *Splendid* (1829–31). Phillip Bridgeo was skipper of the *Sally* (1828–30), the *Quero* (1832–33), and the *William* (1834–36). William D. Hammond was skipper of the *Ploughboy* (1828 and 1830), the *Mechanic* (1829), and the *Sally* (1833), and by 1850 was reputed to be worth $50,000. John S. Peach was skipper of the *Sally* (1834) and the *Marblehead* (1835–38).[42] John White had the *Hope* in 1826–30.

Many skippers probably also aspired to part-ownership of a schooner, but less than 17 percent of all skippers (and a like proportion of those in Marblehead), achieved this.[43] The share system gave skippers an incentive to succeed in a fishing voyage, while the owner had no incentive to give up additional earnings. But ownership of schooners in Marblehead was not concentrated in the hands of just a few owners. Of 51 schooners whose ownership can be ascertained in 1834, Kimball was the only owner with four schooners, although various unassociated (or loosely

associated) Broughton family members owned a total of eight, and the extended
Knight and Martin families owned five each. Most owners owned only one or two
schooners. In order for a skipper to finance a voyage on his own, he would need
not only to pay about $2,000 for a vessel, but also to advance about $500 for great
and small generals and insurance. Such an investment would represent more than
ten years' earnings as a fisherman.

While skippers competed to be associated with an owner, the crew competed
to be associated with a successful skipper. Many crew changed vessels frequently.
This was somewhat less true of Samuel Snow's crews: two men (Joseph Severy
and George Melzard) sailed with Snow on every voyage from 1825 to 1830, and
Benjamin and Peter Severy also sailed with Snow from 1828 to 1830. It is not
clear whether these crewmembers were related to Snow, but they probably were in
some way.

For some reason, in 1831 Snow chose a completely new crew for the three
fares that the schooner *Splendid* sailed that year. But 1831 was to be an unusual
year. The *Marblehead Register* for December 3, 1831, reported: "It may be worthy
of remark, that the oldest citizens among us cannot recollect a season when a large
proportion of [the 'fall faremen'] were not at home on the 1st of Dec." It soon
became clear that the fleet had been caught in a bad storm, as more and more
damaged schooners limped home, with reports such as of seeing "the wreck of a
sch about 50 tons, on her beam ends, with white mast heads, two stump topmasts
painted white, new bowsprit."[44] On January 28, 1832, the *Register* reported that
the schooner *Friend* had been wrecked on the previous November 11, with the loss
of two crew. The rest of the crew remained on the wreck for 58 days until they
were picked up by the ship *Hudson*, of New York. Later, on February 25, 1832, the
paper reported: "There is one fishing vessel missing from this port, the *Splendid*,
Snow." The *Splendid* and its crew never returned, one of six Marblehead fishing
vessels lost at sea in 1831.[45] Lost in the *Splendid* were Samuel Snow, Winslow
Ramsdell, Grush Selman, John D. Dennis, Phillip B. Millet, and John Adams.[46]
Fortunately for their families, most of these men were members of the Marblehead Charitable Society, instituted on February 12 of that same year, and so their
widows or orphans were eligible for relief.[47]

Samuel Snow's brother Thomas and nephew Joseph White Snow continued
the family tradition, Thomas on the schooner *Brilliant*, and Joseph on various
larger vessels.

ENDNOTES

1   The agreement also set forth the duty of the crew, and the penalty for desertion. It did not mention the 10 percent fee for the owner added to the cost of the great and small generals (see Fishing Agreements).

2   Whidden p. 116. Before the Civil War, a share of 1/5 was taken in Maine (Rowe, 1948, p. 271), and 3/10 was taken in the mackerel fishery in Cohasset, Massachusetts, in 1851 (*Harding* v. *Souther*, 66 MA 307, Sup. Ct. MA, 1853—see Morison, 1921, p. 310). An owner's proportion of one-half was taken in Gloucester (Reynolds p. 43; Fishing Agreements; see also *Noble* v. *U.S.*, 1856 U.S. Ct. Cl. 81). Apparently, the owners of the larger French overseas codfishing vessels were entitled to between 2/3 and 3/4 of the profit (Anson, 1931, pp. 69–70, 74). These proportions were uniform within a port in the United States, but were not a large enough factor to induce movement between ports by owners or fishermen.

3   Act of 1813, c. 34, section 5, cited in the cases of the *Harriet* (see this chapter) and *Rich* v. *The Cherub* (see chapter 2 n. 5). Kimball apparently often acted as his own shoreman, as he owned property for fish flakes near Little Harbor in Marblehead.

4   *Harding* v. *Souther* (see n. 2 above), a suit brought by a cook for wages.

5   A principle at issue in *William Bradford* v. *Ellis Drew* (46 MA 188, Sup. Ct. MA, 1842). It is not usually clear from the account book when the fish were sold and the men paid. Fish caught in spring and summer fares may have been cured soon enough for sale in the fall, or the fish might be sold at the end of the fare to someone else to cure. Kimball's account book does not show extensions of credit to fishermen (other than skippers) for purchases from his store, except for the great and small general supplies for a voyage and an occasional advance of the bounty if the fishermen were paid before the end of the year when the bounty was collected (Account book, p. 58—see n. 9 below; Chadwick, 1906, p. 49).

6   McFarland pp. 134–37. The maximum bounty was $360, which probably discouraged building vessels larger than 90 tons (McFarland p. 163).

7   *U.S.* v. *Lindsey Nickerson, Jr.*, 58 U.S. 204 (1854, holding that the defendant could not be tried twice for perjury in connection with an application for bounty).

8   Hind, 1863, pp. 217, 219, 223 and 227. Innis, pp. 183 n.1, 214, and 375. "Between 1817 and 1829 … the bounty paid by France for fish dried and exported from the colony rose more than tenfold…." (Baehre p. 176).

9   This account book, 350 closely packed large pages, is in Kimball's own handwriting, and one can picture him keeping the records in his store, making entries as transactions were made, and showing the book to his crews and others with whom he did business.

It was not a big enough operation to be called a counting house. The account book sets forth accounts of fishing fares, which could be shown to the crews as required by the fishing agreement, and in some cases countersigned by them as acknowledgement that the accounts had been settled. It covers certain voyages (during the years 1825–37) of 12 of Kimball's schooners, and also includes many accounts of other individuals and firms he did business with. Other account books must have been lost.

10 Account book, pp. 57–58. The dates of the fares, and often the number of quintals, are found in the fishing agreements in the National Archives.

11 McFarland (p. 138) reports that from 1824 to 1832, the duty was 20 cents per bushel (there are 6.76 bushels per hogshead). The duty was reduced to 10 cents per bushel in 1832 and 8 cents in 1842. Innis, p. 324. About 12 hogsheads of salt were needed per 100 quintals of fish (Ryan p. 42, and account book). Salt was imported from Salt-Tortuga (the modern-day island of La Tortuga, Venezuela), the Cape Verde Islands, Salt Cay in the Turks Islands (part of today's Turks and Caicos Islands, in the Caribbean), Lisbon, and the Bay of Biscay (McFarland p. 95). In many fishing voyages, the schooner returned for one reason or another before all the salt was wetted, and the remaining salt was credited to the proceeds of the voyage.

12 Account book pp. 13, 17, 19–20, and 57.

13 Account book p. 19. One source quotes $15.50 as the premium for $500 insurance (from the Marblehead Marine Insurance Co.) on a schooner worth $1,000 (Lord and Gamage p. 146).

14 When chartering a vessel, by contrast, the owner usually supplied the captain and crew and paid the insurance, though these expenses were figured into the charter fee.

15 "Because of the lack of charts [of Labrador] ... it was hazardous and many vessels were lost. [The fishing season] of southern and northern Labrador averaged about eighty-seven and fifty-two days, respectively.... It is important to realize that from the beginning, the Labrador fishery was not, by itself, generally remunerative [for Newfoundland boats] and its success depended largely on the seal fishery" (Ryan p. 49). The case of *Rich* v. *The Cherub* (see chapter 2 n. 5) concerned a voyage to Labrador (perhaps meaning the Gulf of St. Lawrence) from Marblehead in 1822. The 79-ton schooner was gone 5 months and returned with 800 quintals of fish and 19 barrels of oil. The 10 fishermen each earned only $40.81 (not including bounty, apparently). It is not clear why Labrador voyages had larger crews.

16 Secondary sources also show considerable differences in the average annual earnings of fishermen at various periods: figures quoted include $200–$300 (Vickers, 1994, p. 273), $214 (McFarland p. 186), or $157 (Morison, 1921, p. 311); they also note that political opposition to the bounty in the United States was quelled by showing that many fishermen only earned $77 per year, bounty included (McFarland p. 163). For a general idea of these amounts in today's dollars, see www.westegg.com/inflation. It

shows that $1 in 1825 was worth $15.98 in 2003, based on consumer price indices. During the period under discussion, consumer prices did not vary much, $1 in 1825 being worth $0.82 in 1860 (after the depression of 1857).

17 *Marblehead Gazette*, April 21, 1832, and February 2, 1833. These articles estimate the average fisherman's earnings as $213.52 for 1831 and $254.58 for 1832, but these estimates do not take account of great-general expenses other than salt and bait, or of the small-general expenses.

18 In the fishing agreements, the owner certified to the facts of the voyage and the catch.

19 The fishing agreement states: "bounty by act of congress June 30, 1834" (VRM gives 1839 rather than 1834). Lost were William Doliber, Sr. and Jr., Thomas R. Woodfin, Samuel and Joseph Davis, and Richard Renew. The Marblehead monument to those lost at sea does not list these men.

20 Assuming a 70 ton vessel with seven fishermen. The 20 cents per bushel on salt (less in later years) for 1000 quintals of fish amounted to $162, or about $15 per fisherman, substantially less than the fisherman's share of the bounty.

21 *North American Review* 120 (1843): 78–81. Regarding the numbers of visiting boats, see the extract from elsewhere in this speech quoted in chapter 2.

22 Morison (1921) p. 311; McFarland p. 163.

23 11 F. Cas. 588, 592 (Cir. Ct. ME, 1840). The decision held that the vessel should be forfeited under the act for fraud in procuring the bounty. Richard Henry Dana, Jr., argued the case for the owners in the District Court (11 F. Cas. 587). The issue of whether a vessel could take other fish without violating its license for the codfishery arose again in *U.S.* v. *The Raindeer* (27 F. Cas. 758, Cir. Ct. R.I., 1848). In that case zealous officers had seized 14 vessels, with 130 men, at anchor in Newport Harbor in bad weather, and attempted to forfeit the vessels for catching mackerel with a cod license. The lengthy statements of Circuit Justice Woodbury in invalidating this seizure resonate today in an era of depleted stocks and fishing quotas:

> [The act] was designed, doubtless, merely to prevent getting bounties, without the training and exposure connected with the codfishery, as a great nursery for seamen. It looked, likewise, to security against bounties being obtained, when fishermen did not bring into the country the additional food and wealth, drawn from the depths of the ocean, in that fishery, and which it was a national object on that account, also to foster; or when they did not labor in competition with rival nations, encouraged by bounties in that fishery, and who would otherwise become triumphant over ourselves, and exclude us entirely from that great mine of riches and nautical skill. . . .
>
> It is not a fault in the vessel if cod do not bite; provided the crew try to catch them, they fulfill their duty....

She may catch mackerel, for instance, for bait, or for food on board ship, any thing which is incidental, merely. But beyond that, if, in doing what is incidental, she happens to strike such large schools, as to pull in more than are so needed at once, it cannot be that she must halt midway in their biting, and refrain to pull in one extra mackerel, or forfeit the whole vessel. That is a kind of self-restraint not to be expected of a fisherman....

From the very nature of ocean fisheries, where so many different kinds of fish abound, and live in the same seas and latitudes, and even on the same feeding grounds, the fisherman is often compelled, in some degree, to take different kinds of fish, whether he seeks them or not. The same hook, bait and line will answer for several different kinds, and till they come to the surface, or are drawn into his boat, the fisherman cannot determine which he has caught.... [C]an the law be so harsh, unless he makes a real and permanent change in his trade or employment, as to punish him with a penalty for catching any thing except cod? As if he derived his right to catch any kind of fish in the ocean from government, instead of god and nature....

On the other hand, a forfeiture was decreed in *U.S.* v. *The Paryntha Davis*, 27 F. Cas. 456 (D.C.D.ME, 1858), where no cod—but 15 barrels of mackerel—were found on board.

24 Innis (1940) p. 285; Vickers (1994) p. 279. The price of the fish in foreign markets is given as $6 per quintal (McFarland p. 153). "The offshore codfishery of 1829 was in a depressed state. The business had become of little value to the owners of the fishing vessels, due largely to competition of foreign fishermen and higher rates of bounty paid to them. The falling off of foreign trade also meant the loss of profitable returns formerly made on cargoes of sugar, wine and other imports, brought by vessels on their return trips from selling their fish abroad" (McFarland p. 192).

25 Roads pp. 272–73; Baehre p. 155.

26 Chadwick (1906).

27 *Ibid.* p. 28.

28 *Ibid.* p. 31.

29 *Ibid.* pp. 37–38. The *Marblehead Gazette* for July 14, 1832, contained an editorial noting that four recently arrived schooners were manned without spirituous liquors, and stated, "The tax for liquors on board our fishermen has been great for the past years, and we believe it altogether necessary."

30 His brother Charles Chadwick died in the *Senator*, his cousin John White died in the *Clinton*, and another cousin, also called John White, died in the *Zela* (VRM, Roads pp. 374–76).

31 Women could also supplement a family income, but no evidence has been found of women on fishing voyages.

32 Reynolds pp. 48 and 112.

33 Room and board included in both cases.

34 Morison (1921) pp. 136–37. The current author does not wish to quibble with historians about their conclusions, but it seems wrong to say that "Fishermen were not used to discipline or to quick movements, and were apt to shy at laying out on yardarms," and to characterize them as "[A] class of men who … would not submit to the wage system, the discipline, and the lengthy voyages of merchant vessels," as Morison does. Wells, who actually went on a fishing voyage, describes the activity when the fishermen encounter a school of mackerel: "When the fish are plentiful, the scene is one of the most exciting that can be imagined. The long, lithe bodies of the fishermen bending eagerly over their work, the quick and nervous twitching at the line, followed by the steady strain, and the rapid hand-over-hand haul that brings the prize to the surface, and the easy swing with which he describes a circle in the air as the victor slaps him into his barrel … it is a sport to which the efforts of the trout angler, or the fowler … are but puny and insignificant in comparison" (Wells p. 468). Many fishing fares were as long as most merchant voyages.

35 The contrast between the egalitarian, communal structure of a fishing crew, and the more hierarchical structure of a merchant crew is reflected in the law applicable to merchant seamen. In a case voiding a provision in shipping articles (the agreement between owner and crew) that conflicted with the right of seamen to their wages when a neutral ship was captured, Circuit Justice Joseph Story explained the need for courts of admiralty to protect the rights of seamen: "Seamen are a class of persons remarkable for their thoughtlessness and improvidence. They are generally necessitous, ignorant of the nature and extent of their own rights and privileges, and for the most part incapable of duly appreciating their value. They combine, in a singular manner, the apparent anomalies of gallantry, extravagance, profusion in expenditure, indifference to the future, credulity, which is easily won, and confidence, which is readily surprised. Hence it is, that bargains between them and shipowners, the latter being persons of great intelligence and shrewdness in business, are deemed open to much observation and scrutiny; for they involve great inequality of knowledge, of forecast, of power, and of condition. Courts of admiralty on this account are accustomed to consider seamen as peculiarly entitled to their protection; so that they have been, by a somewhat bold figure, often said to be favorites of courts of admiralty" (*Brown* v. *Lull*, 4 F. Cas. 407, Cir. Ct. MA, 1836). The decision held that the provision in shipping articles would be held void unless the provision was "fully and fairly" explained to the seamen and additional compensation was paid "entirely adequate to the new restrictions and risks." It involved a capture in 1810 that was not compensated for by the capturing nation until just prior to the case in 1836.

36 Melville chapter 29.

37 Russell Knight, as quoted in Bourne pp. 72–73. Kinship still plays an important role in New England fishing today (Doeringer *et al.*, 1986, pp. 59ff).

38 Account book p. 257. *Rich* v. *The Cherub* (see chapter 2 n. 5) indicates that in Marblehead the skipper has an equal share with his companions, unless otherwise agreed. *Harding v. Souther*, n. 2; *Halsey Baker v. Joseph Corey*, 36 MA 496 (Sup. Ct. MA, 1837).

39 Fishing agreements for 1843 (the *John*), 1844 (the *Quero*), and 1845 (the *John*, *Mt. Vernon*, and *Thomas*). In these situations, a greater fraction of the proceeds remained to be shared by the crew, accommodating the tendency of Labrador voyages to employ larger crews.

40 Tutt p. 13

41 Bourne. In contrast, on pirate voyages, the pirate captain was chosen by the crew, but was still paid a larger share of the loot (Whipple, 1958).

42 According to a brief history of the Peach family in *Marblehead* magazine, "Captain John Peach and his son Captain Thomas Peach served on the fishing fleets from 1832 to 1888 and between the two of them, they amassed 85 years of sea duty. During his 50 years at sea, Captain Thomas made 85 trips to the Grand Banks fishing" (www.legendinc.com/Pages/MarbleheadNet/MM/FirstFamilyFolder/Peaches.html; see also Roads p. 366). A John Peach and a Thomas Peach crewed on the *Garland* as early as 1827.

43 Vickers (1994) pp. 268–69, 280, and 287 n. 38.

44 *Salem Gazette*, December 9, 1831, article headed: "There are now 27 fishing vessels absent from Marblehead." The *Gazette* for December 27 would later report the wreck of the ship *Athens*, Hooper, of Marblehead, on the Bahama Bank in early December.

45 *Marblehead Gazette*, April 21, 1832.

46 VRM. Selman and Adams are not listed on the Fishermen's Monument on Burial Hill in Marblehead, which only lists members of the Charitable Seamen's Society.

47 Marblehead Museum and Historical Society. All but Dennis and Adams were members.

FOUR

THE SCHOONER OWNER:
EDMUND KIMBALL

IN 1807, EDMUND KIMBALL, a 21-year-old housewright, moved to Marblehead. He came from Wenham, a landlocked farming community of 500 located about ten miles away on the other side of Salem and Beverly.[1] He shared business premises with another housewright, Josiah P. Creesy, who had moved to the town from New Hampshire, and their association continued after each turned to the cod-fishery, and until Josiah, "shoreman," died in 1844.[2] One of Josiah's sons, Josiah Jr., born and raised in Marblehead, became the captain of the famous clipper ship *Flying Cloud* on its record-setting voyages from New York to San Francisco, and later retired to Wenham.[3]

Like others during this period, Edmund Kimball's family had many members in seafaring pursuits. His older brother, Paul, had died at sea in 1797 at age 16; his first cousin William Kimball, born in 1772 and residing in Wenham, was a shipmaster, also lost at sea, in 1819; and his uncle, another Edmund Kimball, was a shipowner in Newburyport.[4] Another first cousin, Benjamin Porter, lived in Marblehead and in the 1820s owned several fishing schooners, becoming a prominent merchant.[5]

Edmund Kimball. Portrait by William Bartoll.

During the War of 1812, Edmund Kimball was a captain in the Marblehead militia, and in 1813 he married Mary Hooper, whose mother, Deliverance Knight, and father, Asa Hooper, had been born in Marblehead.[6] Asa was a sea captain and a shipowner in foreign trade. During the war he was captain of the privateer brig *Thorn* when it captured as a prize in 1812 an American vessel, the *Hiram*, that sailed from Baltimore, Maryland, carrying a British safe-conduct license issued by the British consul in Boston protecting it from capture by the British.[7] This prize claim initially was disallowed, but finally was decided in Asa's favor by the Supreme Court in 1814 in a decision that relied on an earlier decision by Justice Joseph Story.[8]

The Marbleheader Joseph Story had a defining impact on maritime law in the United States. The son of Doctor Elisha Story, who had taken part as an "Indian" in the Boston Tea Party, he was educated at Marblehead Academy and Harvard, practiced law in Salem, and served briefly in Congress.[9] In 1812, at age 32, he became the youngest-ever Justice on the U.S. Supreme Court, serving until 1845.[10] As such, he was required to spend much of his time, when the Supreme Court was not hearing arguments, "riding circuit" as a Circuit Justice who sat (together with a local Federal District Court judge) on the Federal Circuit Court in New England, hearing trials and appeals—largely maritime cases.[11] This additional duty meant that he might sometimes decide the same case a second time, if it was appealed to the Supreme Court. As permitted at the time, he also was the president of the Merchants Bank of Salem (beginning in 1814), and a professor and dean at Harvard Law School (1829–45), as well as an active drafter of legislation.[12]

Early in his judicial career, Story decided many cases dealing with admiralty and prize law, which were then unsettled and imperfectly understood.[13] One issue that arose during the War of 1812 was whether an American vessel sailing under a British license was a lawful prize as an enemy vessel for American privateers. Story, as circuit justice, held that an American vessel, the *Julia*, sailing from Baltimore under a British license was a valid prize because it assisted the enemy by delivering goods to the combined British-Spanish armies fighting the French in Spain.[14] An historian notes,

> At the time the war was declared Great Britain was operating extensively against the French on the Iberian Peninsula, and depended largely on America for provisions. High prices for such supplies tempted many of our merchants not only to run the risk of capture and confiscation of their cargoes, but to brave the odium of their fellow-countrymen.[15]

The Supreme Court upheld the decision on appeal in 1814 in an opinion by Story that quoted at length from his own opinion in the circuit court. Chief Justice John Marshall (with whom Story usually agreed), silently dissented.[16]

The owner of Asa Hooper's prize, the *Hiram*, had purchased a license for a fee of one dollar per barrel for as much as the vessel could carry. The same federal district court judge in Boston that a month later would condemn the *Julia* held, with some uncertainty, that the *Hiram* was not a valid prize, but the Supreme Court, on the basis of Story's decision in the Supreme Court in *The Julia*, upheld the validity of the prize.[17] The capture of American vessels by American privateers involved judgment and, in some cases, trickery. The instructions to the captain of the Marblehead private armed schooner *Industry* in August 1813 stated:

> If you fall in with any American vessels from Boston or any other Port, loaded with provisions & cleared for Eastport or any other Port, board her under English Colours, & declare your intention of sending her to Newprovidence, probably he may deliver up his License. If not, & you have reasonable grounds to suspect that he is bound to an enemy's Port or that it's Enemies Property; then rigidly search her – but treat them well, & if you find an English License, or any other papers proving it Enemies property, or that she is bound to an English Port, then send them in for trial to the first Amern. Port. You will bear in mind that *all American vessels bound out with English Licenses* will, if brought in, be good prizes.[18]

The *Industry,* a small schooner of 39 tons, mounted four carriage guns and was crewed by 35 Marbleheaders, some of whom would later be sea captains.[19]

Story had an expansive and activist view of national judicial power. In a leading case in 1815, he held as a circuit justice that federal admiralty jurisdiction extended to maritime insurance cases, contrary to the practice in England, from which America usually derived its law. He traced the history of admiralty from early European decisions, which derived from ancient sea codes, such as those from the Isles of Oleron (off the coast of France in the Atlantic) and Rhodes (in the Mediterranean), the latter dating from before the time of Christ.[20] A principle of maritime law was that, as a form of international law, it should be the same in Rome (and Boston) as in Athens. Story was of the opinion that admiralty jurisdiction should apply to all maritime contract and tort cases. It was not until 1871 that the Supreme Court had occasion to decide this issue, agreeing with Story.[21] Although there was uncertainty in the interim, Story's view became generally accepted, and had wide impact because maritime cases were perhaps half of all commercial litigation at the time.[22] As noted in the *Harvard Law Review*:

> Virtually because of a single man, the scholarly, determined New Englander, Justice Joseph Story, the Federal Courts, in contrast to their English counterparts, gradually came to assert jurisdiction over a broad field of maritime cases.[23]

Because of the importance of a uniform law, admiralty cases must be brought in federal court, and the judge, rather than a jury, decides issues of fact as well as issues of law, although subsequent legislation has provided for jury trials in some cases.

Story used his intimate and sympathetic understanding of seamen and maritime issues, gained from his early experience in Marblehead, to temper some of the rigidities of the ancient Admiralty law.

> Judging from the series of eighteen opinions on seamen's wages handed down on circuit between 1814 and 1845, Story uniformly used [his] discretion to expand the rights of seamen....Paralleling judicial reform in contracts were Story's [legislative] efforts to abolish flogging and other harsh punishments that traditionally had been unquestioned but that worked to diminish the seaman's general status as a free bargaining agent.[24]

As an example, in a Marblehead case brought by a crewmember on the brig *Polly* against the Hooper owner to recover wages the seaman had lost when the vessel was captured by the Danes in 1809, Story held that the seaman was entitled to recover full wages when the owner received reparations from the Danish

Government in 1830, even though the reparations were only in the amount of one third of the freight.

> The seamen's wages generally constitute a lien, or claim upon the ship and freight, and upon the proceeds thereof, in whatever hands they may be, which must be paid before any other claims. It has been significantly said, that they are nailed to the last plank of the ship; a figurative expression, which will be found used in one of the earliest maritime codes in modern times (the Consolato del Mare [dating from the 11th-13th centuries]) of which we have any distinct traces.[25]

In addition to a sympathetic understanding of maritime issues, and a far-ranging scholarship, Story's opinions employ—not least of all—vivid language. In a case involving the degree to which seamen's wages should be forfeited for committing a revolt on a Marblehead ship owned by the Hoopers, he wrote:

> It need hardly be stated, that in [admiralty] court, seamen, as a class of persons, are entitled to receive particular indulgence. Their habits of life, their incessant and laborious service, their frequent exposure to peril of no ordinary character, their intrepidity and thoughtlessness, their hardihood, sometimes approaching almost from necessity to ferocity, and their profuse and often captivating gallantry, give a coloring to their characters so mixed and variable, so full of lights and shades, that it requires the intimate knowledge of a court of admiralty duly to estimate both their frailties and their merits. They partake, in short, somewhat of the boisterousness of the element which they navigate; and their acts must be judged of, not by the courtesy, or the rigid exactions of domestic society, but by that milder judgment, which winks at their errors, and mitigates its own resentment in consideration of the provocations, temptations, and personal infirmities incident to their employment. To visit all their ill-advised, and even mischievous conduct with severe penalties, would be most discouraging to the maritime service of the country, and perhaps fatal to the safety, as well as the enterprise of our commerce. To indulge them in gross misdemeanors, without adequate correction, would be to create mutinies, and overturn the discipline of the ship, and thereby open a path to the destruction, both of the property and of the persons on board. The marine law has therefore, in cases of this nature, adopted a milder course. It punishes gross and obstinate offences with a forfeiture of wages, especially if they are persisted in without repentance or amends. It treats lighter faults with an indulgent lenity, allowing compensation for any losses and expenses caused by them; passing over slight errors, unaccompanied with mischief, without notice; and correcting habitual neglect, or incompetent performance of duty, when it

Lydia Russell Kimball. Portrait by William Bartoll.

amounts only to levissima culpa by a correspondent diminution of wages.[26]

Marblehead had 78 schooners fishing for cod in 1817, when Edmund Kimball bought his first schooner. He also participated in Marblehead's foreign trade on vessels owned by Asa Hooper and others.[27] He was concentrating his activities on the ownership of fishing schooners by 1825, when he sent at least five schooners to the banks for cod.[28] On April 18, 1826, his wife Mary bore a sixth child, Sally Leach, but the child died on May 8 the same year, followed by Mary herself on May 15, of consumption. Two and a half years later, Kimball, aged 42 and with five surviving children in tow, married Lydia Mugford Russell, 26 years old, whose father, Captain John Roads Russell, was a captain of schooners engaged in foreign trade.[29] Soon after Edmund and Lydia's marriage, on May 1, 1829, Edmund's son William died "by falling down a Schooner's hold" at age 7. Edmund and Lydia's first child together, born shortly afterward on July 20, 1829, was named William Porter Kimball in memory of Edmund's lost son. Lydia and Edmund would have seven other children.[30] In addition to their house at 8 Washington Square, Kimball acquired business premises facing the harbor on Front Street, a wharf at the foot of State Street, and land for fish flakes on Little Harbor.[31]

In 1826, Kimball sent out eight vessels, and four other owners sent out four schooners each (Joseph W. Green, Nicholas Broughton, William Brown, and John Gregory).[32] Kimball employed between four and eight schooners in the codfishery during each of the years 1825 through 1840, employing about 50 fishermen.[33] For an owner, losses of vessels were insured, and income was assured as long as the fish kept biting. Kimball usually sold his fish locally to Porter & Green, prominent merchants catering to the fishing industry, of which his cousin was a partner.[34] It was during this period, and primarily in this repetitive business, that he accumulated his fortune. His profit as an owner of schooners is not computed in his account book, but it can be estimated that he earned enough to pay off the cost of a schooner (about $2,000 for a mix of new and used vessels) over three or four years.[35] Of the 30 schooners that Kimball owned over his career (they are listed in Appendix C), he bought only eight of them new.[36] Some were quite old when acquired (such as the *Ploughboy*, 23 years, or the *Sally*, 28 years), so they must have been well cared for. His period of ownership varied, the longest being of the *America*, which he owned for 24 years. Many of his schooners were registered for foreign trade, and made foreign trading voyages, or were employed in other ways.[37]

Edmund appears to have named most of his new schooners for members of his family who had died, such as his son William (the first of that name), his brother John, and his son Thomas. Later, many of the bigger vessels that he had built for him were named for living family members. One used schooner he bought, the *Quero*, was named for one of the fishing banks, Banquereau, off Cape Breton, Nova Scotia.

Except for shipbuilding, Marblehead was self-sufficient in most of the businesses needed to support the fishing industry. It had sailmakers, ropemakers, boatbuilders to repair vessels, an insurance company, merchants who would market the fish, and many other supportive trades. The fishing schooners used in Marblehead had evolved in their design from the "heeltappers," "pinkys," and "dogbodies" to the vessels of this period that had square sterns (seen from above) and still rather bluff bows. Most of those used in Marblehead were built to the north, in Essex, Danvers, or on the Merrimack River at Newbury, Amesbury, or Salisbury; some were built in Maine or elsewhere.

The principal builders in Essex during the period 1816–40 were the Storys and the Burnhams, who are still building replicas of fishing schooners today.[38] "Essex built about 3,500 registered vessels according to United States Custom House records."[39] "[W]ith hand tools, Essex builders could build vessels rapidly. One builder, in 1856–57, built twenty-two vessels in twenty-two months."[40]

Kimball and other merchants (including Joseph W. Green, Benjamin Porter, Knott Martin, and Edmund Bray) seem to have been dissatisfied with the banking facilities provided in the town by the Marblehead Bank (founded in 1804), since in 1831 they founded the aptly named Grand Bank (remarkably, still existing as an independent bank) to provide competition, and cater to the fishing industry.[41] Green, who had been an owner of fishing schooners and trading brigs and a partner in Porter & Green, was the first president of the bank.[42] During the financial panic of 1837, Green had personal financial difficulties, and Kimball obtained a judgment against him, acquiring two schooners (the *Science* and the *Charlotte*) and other property; Green resigned as president of the bank.[43]

Where his own money was concerned, Kimball could be unforgiving. One observer at the time describes another schooner owner as "kind-hearted," but goes on to state: "He had all their earnings in his hands, and paid for them in goods at his own price, and how could he fail but grow rich, or they to remain poor?"[44] The credit report on Edmund Kimball by Dun & Co. (the predecessor of Dun & Bradstreet) for March 1847 has: "Rich and mean as can be."[45] He certainly seems to have been tight. He found it necessary to identify as "goodwill" a 20 cent credit to the account of one of his best skippers in order to balance the account.[46]

ENDNOTES

1   Two contracts for the construction of houses by Edmund in 1821 are recorded at the Salem Registry of Deeds, book 224, pp. 302–03. One is located at 19 Mechanic St.

2   Deed of land near Redd's Pond dated 1816 to Edmund and Josiah, "both of Marblehead, housewrights" at book 208, p. 287. A recent book describes Josiah as "a wealthy architect and builder in the lumber business," and as a Freemason (Shaw, 2000, pp. 14–15). Deed of a store on State St. dated 1834 to Edmund and Josiah, book 276, p. 211, and Edmund's account book, pp. 18, 133, 159, 177, 306, and 308. Josiah bought the schooners *Hope* and *Ploughboy* from Edmund in 1831.

3   This sailing record, 89 days and 8 hours, anchor to anchor via Cape Horn, stood until recently. It was no fluke of the weather, as the ship made another voyage in 89 days 21 hours, as well as a record voyage to Hong Kong (Howe *et al.* pp. 190–95).

4   Morrison and Sharples (1897), pp. 226, 418. When William was only one year old, his parents "with eight others drowned June 17, 1773, by the sinking of a boat off Salem Harbor." Porter (1878), pp. 310-1. Edmund Kimball of Newburyport (a port on the Merrimac River roughly twenty miles north of Marblehead) was a prominent shipowner there during the period 1786-1826. His vessels (he owned 25 during his career) were mostly ships and brigantines under 100 feet and 100-300 tons, a common size for the period. They were engaged in overseas trade, including carrying salt cod to Europe and the West Indies, and salt and other cargoes on the return. Uncle Edmund had commanded the brigs Speedwell, Molly and Betsey. Bayley and Jones (1906), pp. 79, 359. However, no direct business connection has been found with his nephew Edmund. The Phillips Library has 13 boxes of his records. Manuscript # 80.

5   Benjamin was born in 1786, like Edmund. Porter, pp. 256-7, 278, 281, 308, 310-1, and 327. The Kimball and Porter families were closely related by marriage, which often happened at the time. In addition to his father, Edmund's aunt Mary, uncle Edmund, first cousin William, and sister Clarissa all married Porters.

6   A letter he drafted in 1876, when he was 89, to one of his relatives, recalls his war service: "I went to Marblehead in 1807 and with some of the young men formed a company of infantry in 1812. I had a commission from Gov. Caleb Strong as Captain of a company of artillery. I was under the Mayor as a coast defense to set the guard and give them the counter-sign. Marblehead harbor lays open to the sea and the water is very deep and easy of access for the British ship of war. The people were much alarmed lest the town be burned by the warship. We could see the British ship Shannon when she took the Chesapeake. I think I served more than 60 days as we had to repair and strengthen the two fortresses on the harbor on the Marblehead side." Phillips Library, manuscript with excerpts from log of Anna Kimball 1864a, microfilm 91, roll 56. Mary was a Beverly Hooper and not a descendent of the Marblehead clan. Pope

(1908), p. 197. Apparently, there was not a common ancestor of the two clans in this country.

7   He was also a representative in the state legislature (Lindsey, 1915, p. 77). The Hoopers apparently lived at 5 Washington Street in a house built by Asa's father, William, in about 1780, and Edmund and Mary may have lived there at first (Lord and Gamage p. 255).

8   *The Hiram, Barker, Master*, 12 U.S. 444 (1814); see also *Hooper et al. v. The Hiram*, 12 Fed. Cas. 469 (D. MA, 1813) and The *Hiram—Cornthwait et al.*, 14 U.S. 440 (1816). The bond of Asa Hooper as a privateer is printed on p. 76 of Lindsey. Under the law of prize at the time, the owner of the *Thorn* was entitled to half of the proceeds under the Act of Congress of June 26, 1812, the balance to be shared among the crew under the Act of April 23, 1800, unless there was an agreement to the contrary. The *Dos Hermanos*, appendix, 15 U.S. 76 (1817). The 1800 Act, 2 Stat. 52, section 6(I), provided that the master (Hooper) was entitled to 3/20 of the balance. The *Hiram* was captured by the *Thorn* on October 15, 1812, but in November of 1812, William Bentley's diary says, "We have news of capture of the *Thorn*, privateer from Marblehead, by a British frigate. She carried 16 guns, & 140 men, & was pronounced an excellent brig." Bentley, vol. IV, p. 134. It is not known whether Hooper was captured with the *Thorn*.

9   Marblehead Academy taught Latin and Greek, as well as other subjects, and admitted girls on the same footing as boys (Roads pp. 260–62 and 497).

10 Dunne (1970) p. 91.

11 Dunne pp. 96–97, 253–54.

12 Dunne pp. 121, 141–43, 268, and 328. One of the laws he drafted made cruelty to seamen a crime (Mudgett).

13 Story pp. 222–24.

14 *The Julia*, 14 Fed. Cas. 31 (Cir. Ct. MA, 1813) (Maclay pp. 242–48).

15 Maclay p. 242. See also Dunne p. 107.

16 *The Julia*, 12 U.S. 181 (1814). See also Dunne pp. 107 and 114.

17 *The Hiram, Barker, Master*, see note 8 above. The Supreme Court overruled the lower court decisions in this case. Judge Davis held that the *Hiram* was not a valid prize on February 6, 1813, stating: "I should not be surprised if my conclusions should be found erroneous, in which case they will be corrected by a superior tribunal," and on March 9, 1813, he decided that the *Julia* was a valid prize, based on differences of facts in the cases, differences that the Supreme Court found to be irrelevant. It is not clear whether Story was involved as circuit justice in Asa Hooper's case, where a "pro forma decree of affirmance" was made by the Circuit Court, as the Supreme Court records could not be found. In another prize case, Story the teacher took the unusual step of

attaching to his opinion for the Supreme Court a 78-page procedural guide to prize cases (*The Dos Hermanos*, 15 U. S. 76, 1817). This appendix was expanded in *The London Packet*, 15 U.S. 371 (1817).

18 Letter dated August 11, 1813, to Captain Thomas Rice from owners John R. Russell and Aaron Breed (John R. Russell file, Marblehead Museum and Historical Society). The letter also stated: "You will not trouble any vessel from Lisbon, or [Gallvi?] or any other Neutral Port as we may thereby incur much trouble and expense." John Roads Russell would become Edmund Kimball's father-in-law upon the latter's second marriage.

19 Commission to the Industry from President James Madison dated August 9, 1813, in Russell file. This privateer (or another of the same name) had captured the British brig Mary of 266 tons on October 14, 1812, and included as crew Lewis Russell (19 years old) and Samuel Tucker (34 years old). Lindsey, pp. 111, 125; Roads, p. 310.

20 *De Lovio v. Boit*, 7 Fed. Cas. 418 (Cir. Ct. MA, 1815) (Dunne, pp. 129–31). In English law the jurisdiction of Admiralty courts had been limited by legislation for political reasons.

21 *Ins. Co. v. Dunham*, 78 U.S. 1 (1871).

22 See *The Schooner Volunteer*, 1 Sumner 551 (Cir. Ct. D. MA, 1835), reiterating Story's conclusion in *De Lovio*; *Gloucester Ins. Co. v. Younger*, 10 F. Cas. 495 (1855); Flanders (1852) pp. 131–33; and Dunne p. 101.

23 Harvard Law Review (1954). Because Story believed the Constitution gives exclusive authority over maritime matters to the federal government, state statutes could not apply to maritime matters, whether or not Congress had passed a law on the subject. In *The Chusan*, 5 F. Cas. 680 (Cir. Ct. MA, 1843), for example, Story as circuit justice held that a lien under New York law on a Marblehead vessel for materials supplied is invalid under the federal admiralty power. "The subject-matter of admiralty and maritime law is withdrawn from state legislation, and belongs exclusively to the national government and its proper functionaries" (at p. 682). This applies also to "the prescribing of rules for the shipping of seamen." On the other hand, in his *Commentaries on the Constitution* (1833), section 1666, Story states: "It may be added, that, in many of the cases included in these latter classes [maritime commerce], the same reasons [generally, international uniformity] do not exist, as in cases of prize, for an exclusive jurisdiction; and, therefore, whenever the common law is competent to give a remedy in the state courts, they may retain their accustomed concurrent jurisdiction in the administration of it." Edmund Kimball would have occasion to appreciate the exclusiveness of federal admiralty jurisdiction, however, in a case brought against his ship *Anna Kimball*. In 1859, the *Anna Kimball* turned down the services of a pilot when entering San Francisco Bay. The pilot sued the ship in the admiralty jurisdiction of the federal court under a California statute that allowed it to recover half the pilotage

fee when its services were turned down. The court held that admiralty jurisdiction did not extend to liens created by state laws or internal commerce (*Harrison v. The Anna Kimball*, 11 F. Cas. 646, D.C.N.D. Cal. 1859). Among other admiralty cases, Story wrote the politically important opinion for the Supreme Court in *The Amistad*, holding that Africans, who had mutinied and controlled a Spanish slave ship when it was captured as a prize, were freemen who should be liberated, and not cargo (15 Peters 518, 1841; Dunne pp. 395–98).

24 Newmyer (1985), pp. 151-2. The cases cited by Newmyer involved merchant seamen, rather than fishermen. However, Story's view that the Admiralty clause in the Constitution preempted state laws, including state legislation protective of seamen, was criticized by Richard Henry Dana, Jr., who otherwise was a great admirer of his former teacher (Dunne pp. 416 and 433; Mudgett).

25 *Pitman v. Hooper*, 19 F. Cas. 730, (Cir. Ct. MA, 1837); *Pitman v. Hooper*, 19 F. Cas. 737, (Cir. Ct. MA, 1838).

26 *The Mentor*, 17 F. Cas. 15 (Cir. Ct. MA, 1825). The *Mentor* had been on a voyage from Boston to the Sandwich Islands (Hawaii), the Northwest Coast of North America, Canton, and Boston. Story cited the severe old maritime laws and observed that "the milder spirit of modern times has introduced principles, which appear to me more fitted to preserve good order on board."

27 In 1819 he was a consignee with his father-in-law Asa Hooper and others of a shipment of molasses and sugar from Martinique on the Brig *Ardent*, owned by Hooper. In 1820 he was a consignee with some Hoopers and others of more molasses and sugar from Martinique on the schooner *Four Sisters* (Bradlee p. 91). The registry records show that both the *Ardent* and the *Four Sisters*, built in Newburyport in 1816, were schooners altered to brigs, presumably for the foreign trade. A square-rigged brig was more suitable for the varied conditions of ocean voyages.

28 Fishing agreements.

29 He "was with General Henry Knox and Captain Wm Blacker in the boat that ferried General Washington across the Delaware the night before the battle of Trenton (Lindsey p. 111; Lord and Gamage pp. 121–22; Morison, 1921, p. 216 n). His statue now stands at the foot of the battle monument in Trenton. Lydia's great grandfather, Louis Russell (1700–1793), was a French Huguenot who had come to the United States alone as a young person, and had moved to Marblehead to join the substantial French population there (Louis Russell genealogy, Marblehead Museum and Historical Society; see also www.worldconnect.rootsweb.com). Lydia's mother, Elizabeth Mugford, was the half sister of Captain James Mugford, Jr., who, as a newly appointed captain of the schooner *Franklin* in 1776, captured the armed British transport ship *Hope*, laden with 1,500 barrels of gunpowder and other equipment for the British army, and died defending the *Franklin* (Maclay p. 65; Lord and Gamage p. 113).

30 A total of 10 out of Edmund's 14 children lived to maturity. Most of them went to secondary school at Atkinson Academy in Atkinson, NH, where the principal was their aunt Betsy Kimball's son, William C. Todd. The eldest, Edmund Jr., "was a student at Bowdoin college in 1837," and John Russell Kimball "was graduated A.B. at Dartmouth College, 1855." Morrison and Sharples p. 740.

31 The house had been built by John Cross in 1803–04 (Salem Registry of Deeds, book 172, p. 268). Captain Cross was subsequently "with all on board lost at sea in the *Traveller*" in 1804 at age 36. A succession of documents shows how Kimball gradually acquired, and later disposed of, some of this property portfolio:

    In 1823, a deed from Elias Hulen for fish house and fish flakes on Little Harbor, near the fort (Salem Registry, book 233, p. 248).

    In 1826, for $100, a deed from Hannah Glover of all her interest as an heir of Col. Jonathan Glover in "all that wharf … formerly belonging to my said grandfather, Colonel Glover."

    In 1830, a deed from Abigail Robinson for the wharf of Jonathan Glover (Salem Registry, book 255, p. 206).

    In 1834, a deed from Mary Crocker, admin., of 3/5 of a wharf and flats on Front St., between Hooper's wharf and dock and Blackler's wharf and dock (Book 1656, p. 284; see also book 638, p. 44 and book 350, p. 61).

    In 1837, an execution on a judgment obtained by Edmund on a mortgage for $2,752 against Joseph W. Green, merchant, against six listed properties. It is likely that Edmund never took title to most of this, which if sold would probably have exceeded the judgment amount (Account book, p. 78; deed at Book 297, p. 228).

    In 1841, a mortgage deed from Edmund to another for $900 of "all my wharf situation … on Front Street … on [Hooper Wharf and Dock] … on [Blackler Wharf and Dock].

    In 1862, a deed from Edmund of land on Front St., Hooper's wharf and dock, and Blackler's wharf and dock (Salem Registry, book 638, p. 44).

    Edmund had rather extensive real estate dealings throughout his career, in both Marblehead and Wenham.

32 This assumes that the fishing agreements are complete and that the person certifying to the agreements in each case was the owner. Edmund's agreements for 1826 were for the *Enterprise* (sloop, 25 tons), *Alonzo* (40 tons) *Alciope* (36 tons), *Eliza*, *Plough Boy*, *Hope*, *Garland*, and *Mechanic*. The first three were small vessels that apparently were not registered to Edmund, although the account book contains a record of the *Alciope* (p. 17).

33 Account book pp. 33, 168, 220, 263, 307, 345 etc.

34 Account book p. 205, passim. They were general merchants with a wharf at the foot of Water St. in Marblehead (Bradlee p. 141; Roads p. 499). The account book (p. 226)

shows only one foreign voyage to sell fish (to the West Indies, by the schooner *William* in 1837).

35   This works out at an average cost of $35 per register ton (McFarland p. 153; Chapelle p. 78). His revenue from the fishing voyages of four schooners in 1826 was $624 per schooner; for 1827, $686 (five schooners); and for 1828, $529 (seven schooners) — an average of $613 per vessel per year over those three years. After insurance (about $30) and maintenance costs (at least $50 — such as payments to sailmakers, blacksmiths, and for annual caulking and tarring), this would leave some $530 per vessel, though substantial repairs were additional (Marblehead Marine Ins. Co. records).

36   The appendix is based on an abstract of registry records, so it does not necessarily reflect the full extent of Kimball's ownership, since registration was not compulsory. "The registry acts … do not change the common law mode in which ships may be transferred…. In the United States, no vessels are *required* to be registered. But to entitle them to the privileges of vessels of the United States, they must be registered; otherwise, they are deemed alien ships" (Blunt, 1837, pp. 2, 10–11).

37   Abstract of imports and boarding officers' record of arrivals, National Archives and Records Administration record group 036, 20/10/02-5. Some of the schooners may have been chartered, or Edmund may only have owned a mortgage on them from the beneficial owner, who employed them elsewhere.

38   Dana A. Story (1995) p. 45. See also www.essexshipbuildingmuseum.org.

39   Chapelle p. 116.

40   *Ibid.* p. 78.

41   Roads, p. 331; Lord and Gamage pp. 146, 165; *Marblehead Messenger*. Edmund remained a director until at least 1848 (*Marblehead Mercury*, October 20, 1848).

42   Bradlee; Account book pp. 205 and 226.

43   *Marblehead Messenger*. See also *William F. Weld v. James Oliver*, 38 MA 559 (1839), involving Green's ownership of the ship *Senator* and stock of the Grand Bank during the panic.

44   Reynolds, pp. 30–31, 75.

45   Massachusetts, vol. 21, p. 182, R.G. Dun & Co. Collection, Baker Library, Harvard Business School.

46   Account of Phillip Bridgeo, Account book p. 270.

FIVE

THE CODFISHING DECLINE, 1835–46

IN 1835 AND SUBSEQUENT YEARS, MARBLEHEAD SCHOONERS were fishing in much the same way as before, except that more schooners made only one fare.[1] Earnings were somewhat higher than ten years earlier, because the price of fish was at the higher end of the scale, though there was great variation in the catches, from 700 to 1,500 quintals. The *Sally* (62 feet, six men, one fare) earned $105 per man in 1835, but $155 per man (only two of the same men) for 760 quintals in 1836. The *Quero* (63 feet, six men, two fares) earned $208 per man in 1835, and the *Marblehead* (68 feet, nine men, one fare) earned $159 per man in that year.[2] The *William*, skippered by Philip Bridgeo (69 feet, seven or eight men, one fare), was the most profitable, earning $226 per man in 1835, and $165 for 700 quintals in 1836. The earnings still varied greatly. The owner's estimated profit also was greater in 1835–36.[3]

In 1839, the number of Marblehead schooners reached a postwar peak of 85 or more, only three of which went to Labrador and the rest to the Grand Banks.[4] This peak in numbers probably resulted from optimism about the high profits

Pedrick's Warehouse aka Tucker's Wharf, 1891. Courtesy of Historic New England/ SPNEA.

of the mid-1830s, notwithstanding the depressed financial conditions following the financial panic of 1837. But this peak preceded a sharp fall in profits. In 1844 and 1845, the owner's share decreased to 1/4, and the catches were much smaller (500–700 quintals each for three schooners), which must have adversely affected profits. The decrease in the owner's share must have resulted from negotiation with the skipper based on larger crew size (10 men each for two schooners). Fishing became unattractive for both owner and crew, and the number of schooners decreased. There is evidence that cod were becoming scarce, which may have been because of one of the several "prolonged periods of comparative scarcity" of cod that took place in the 1860s, the 1890s, and the 1930s; overfishing may also have begun to take its toll.[5]

Philip Bridgeo, Edmund Kimball's longest-serving skipper, had been born in 1782 and skippered schooners before and after the War of 1812. He skippered Kimball's schooners from 1828–36, and again later, and was part owner of the *Sophonia*. His crews varied greatly, but his son, William Goodwin Bridgeo, began to sail with him as a boy of 17 in 1829, and in 1834 took over as skipper of the *Quero*. William (as well as his cousin George Bridgeo) later died in the hurricane of 1846. Philip's younger son John began sailing with him as a boy of 13 in 1834 on the *William*, and Kimball's son Thomas (aged 18) was also a crewmember on the *William* that year.[6]

Philip was a very good fisherman. His average earnings during his eight consecutive years with Kimball, as reflected in the account book—$193 per year—were higher than the highest average earnings of Kimball's other skippers ($184 per year); only one other skipper beat him more than one year.[7] However, he could not avoid the fluctuation in earnings inevitable in the fisherman's life. His earnings varied from a low of $103 on the *Sally* in 1829 (a generally poor year), to a high of $262 the next year. He continued to skipper Kimball's schooners off and on until 1844, at age 61. The *Boston Shipping List* for July 10, 1844, under "Disasters &c." reports:

> Loss of sch *William*, of Marblehead and two lives. The French brig *Jenne Lodovic*, from Port au Prince for Havre, put into New York 5th inst., for water and provisions, and to land the first officer, four seamen of sch *Marblehead* [sic], and Messrs. C. Gelston and G. W. Reed, passengers. The *William* was on her passage from Miragoane, St. Domingo [now in Haiti] to Boston, and on the 11th ult., at 6 p.m. off Cape Nichol in Mole [now Cape Môle, Haiti] was struck by a white squall,[8] and immediately filled. Capt. Bridgeo and a seaman named Grosvenor Williams were drowned. The others floated on boards and spars until midnight, when they found the boat, and drifted about in her until picked up by the J. L., in lat 20 ½, lon 76. It is not stated how long they were in the boat, but when picked up they were nearly exhausted. Messrs. Gelston & Reed were merchants at Miragoane, and the cargo belonged to them chiefly — it was fully insured in this city. The vessel was worth about $1,000.
>
> Sch William was valued at $2,000, and insured in this city for $1,000.

John Bridgeo would later continue the family tradition as a sea captain on Marblehead ships owned by Kimball and others.

By 1846, the number of Marblehead schooners had declined to 52, and Edmund Kimball only employed two.[9] In September that year a powerful hurricane made its way up the east coast, destroying scores of vessels on its way.[10] By the time it reached the Grand Banks, it must have lost some of its power, but in that shallow water and with a cross sea it was truly devastating. It may have joined

with other storm systems to create a "perfect storm."[11] On September 19, 1846,
it claimed 63 Marblehead fishermen and 11 Marblehead schooners on the banks,
more than 20 percent of the fleet.[12] As one survivor put it: "No tongue can describe
the agonizing fear that beset us all during the hours in which we were compelled to
sit idly in that cabin, silently awaiting what seemed inevitable destruction."

Chadwick describes the devastation on the Banks, and the impact of the trag-
edy on the town.

> The next morning [on the Banks] proof of the mischief wrought
> appeared and multiplied from hour to hour. For days [the schooner]
> sailed through wreckage of all sorts strewing the bank from side to side,
> here some great schooner on her beam ends but not dismasted, lifting
> her masts high out of the water and then again submerging them with a
> most melancholy sound; once the masts of two vessels keeping miserable
> company; objects too easily identified as the belongings of old shipmates,
> relatives and friends.... When the first news of the storm was brought
> [to Marblehead], vague terror seized the town, and only very gradually
> the returning vessels gave to some assurance of surviving friends, and to
> others sadder doubt or certain woe.... [T]he September gale went far
> to spoil [the fishermen's] pleasure in the treacherous sea, and gave the
> fisheries of Marblehead a serious if not fatal shock.[13]

There had always been cordwainers (shoemakers) in Marblehead, but in the
early 19th century shoemaking began to be performed for markets outside the
town, in small accessory buildings known as ten-footers (10' × 10'). By the 1840s,
"... eleven hundred Marbleheaders produce[d] annually over a million pairs of
shoes, worth twice the average catch of the fishing fleet."[14] Some 655 women and
503 men were engaged in making (primarily women's) shoes in 1837, and at the
same time that its fishing fleet reached its peak, Marblehead was the third-biggest
producer of shoes in Massachusetts after Lynn (south of Marblehead, on the other
side of Swampscott) and Haverhill (on the Merrimack River).[15] Women, who
usually worked in the home, stitched together the upper part of the shoe, while
the men, who worked in more than a hundred ten-footers, attached the upper to
the soles.[16] As in the fishing industry, there were owners to be reckoned with: "In
1832, the *Lynn Mirror* reported that of 582 shoemakers in nearby Marblehead,
432 worked for Lynn bosses." The so-called "bosses" supplied the raw materials
and owned the finished product, for which they paid a price to the shoemaker.[17] By
the late 1840s, Marbleheaders had begun to build factories for shoemaking.[18]

From the point of view of the fishermen, it is tempting to see a logic in the transition from codfishing to shoemaking: each was an independent, piecework, meditative occupation, carried on in an isolated location, surrounded primarily by one's relatives and friends. Even the arm motion was similar: "…each bench [was] placed far enough from the wall or the next bench to allow the arms to be swung out as the shoemaker sewed with full length thread. Such a space was called a berth, and the group of men who worked there was called the shop's crew."[19] One observer related:

> The old settlers in Lynn who came from Marblehead, and there were many such here, called these [shoemakers'] aprons "barvels" (pronounced "borvul"). Most of these workmen were fishermen in early life who made their summer trip to the "grand banks," or up the "straits"— and employed the winters at working at the "craft." The "barvel" was a short apron worn to protect the knees from the splashing of water in washing out the fish preparatory to curing them or dry them upon the "flakes." As might be supposed, there were a good many sea phrases, or "salt notes," as they were called, used in the shops.[20]

Meanwhile, Gloucester began to succeed Marblehead as the principal fishing port of the region. It presented a sharp contrast in the composition of its fishing fleet and its practices. In 1834, for example, Gloucester had 46 vessels involved in the codfishery, all under 70 tons, whereas Marblehead had 60 schooners, almost all over 70 tons. The smaller Gloucester vessels had smaller crews (an average of 4–5 men) and sailed less far on more frequent fares (an average of 4–5 fares per year), compared with Marblehead's more uniform seven men and one or two fares to the Grand Banks per year. The Gloucester vessels also caught substantially fewer fish per year (about 300 quintals, compared to Marblehead's roughly 700 quintals), and the earnings must have been substantially less per man, especially after the deduction of the uniform owner's share, which was 1/2 of the proceeds in Gloucester, compared to the 3/8 taken by owners in Marblehead. Even today, the owner of Gloucester swordfishing boats takes ½ the proceeds.[21] In addition to codfishing, however, Gloucester was involved in the mackerel and halibut fisheries.[22] "Mackerelling is often called a lottery. But then there are higher prices in it than in codfishing, if there are more blanks."[23] It was this willingness to pursue different types of fishery that eventually enabled Gloucester to surpass Marblehead as the principal fishing port. Marbleheaders, meanwhile, pursued more lucrative and dependable options such as shoemaking and factory work.[24]

As Chadwick recalls:

"WHEN I WAS WITH SNOW, IN THE 'BRILLIANT.'"

From 49 Harpers New Monthly Magazine, July 1874, page 193.

[The ten-footers] offered great facilities for conversation, though when all were hammering at once, the voices were pitched very high.... Sometimes all talk at once. "When I was with Snow, in the *Brilliant*," one begins; but some heavier engine throws him off the track. He soon gets on again, and begins afresh his story in a higher key, only to be again suppressed. They have all heard it scores and scores of times.[25]

Although Roads says that "no one regrets the passing away of the industry," it is difficult to believe that those that stayed ashore did not miss the good times – the excitement of a good day of fishing or a fast day of sailing, the beauty of the sea in its generous moods, or the welcome home by family and friends.[26]

Endnotes

1   The fishing agreements for 1835 are missing, but in 1834, of 60 schooners that went to the banks from Marblehead, 44 made two fares and 11 made one fare.

2   In 1836, the *Marblehead* (skippered by John Peach) caught 1,221 quintals, and the *Edward* (skippered by Edward Dixey) caught 1,592 quintals (both made two fares). There are no accounts for the *Edward* and *Marblehead* for 1836 in the account book, probably because the book was running out of space.

3   Kimball's average total revenue in 1835 was $932 per schooner; and in 1836, $801. Insurance and maintenance expenses were probably about the same as in 1826–28. Even if we assume that the 10 percent added to the great and small generals for the owner covered normal expenses, the profits were $854 per schooner in 1835 and $725 in 1836.

4   "List of Vessels engaged in the fishing business, owned in Marblehead," *Salem Evening Mercury*, June 19, 1839. Edmund only had the *Quero* in that year. Of the three owners with four or more schooners, two were partnerships (William Thorner had four, Bowden and Goodwin five, and Hooper and Wilson six). Hannah Martin owned two schooners with her son Peter.

5   Harris (1993). "Fishing mortality rates may have exceeded sustainable levels as early as the early 19th century." Hutchings (1993).

6   Account book pp. 194 and 353.

7   William Hammond of the *Ploughboy*, in 1828 and 1830. Philip Bridgeo was the highest-earning skipper in four out of eight years, and in one of those years he was outearned only by his son William on the *Quero*.

8   A white squall means a squall without clouds — perhaps what is now called a microburst.

9   Edmund only owned some four fishing schooners in 1845, and in 1846 he sent only the *Elizabeth* and the *Quero* to the banks. Of these, only *Elizabeth* was on the banks at the time of the hurricane that year, and she survived (Fishing agreements).

10   Boston Shipping List, September 12, 16, 19, 23, 26, 30, and October 3, 7, 10, 14, 21, 24, 1846. The Marblehead schooners lost are not reported there, but ashore at Cape May, NJ, in another gale on October 13 was the "Brig Harriet, of Marblehead, Russell (late Mangan, who was lost overboard Sept. 26) from Campeachy [Campeche, Mexico] for New York, with logwood.... She is owned by Eben Hooper, Esq, Marblehead." Another hurricane hit Cuba and the Florida Keys on October 10–12, 1846 (Boston Shipping List, November 4,7, 1846), when losses from the September hurricane were still being reported. The web site of the Tropical Prediction Center,

National Hurricane Center, National Weather Service lists the "Deadliest Atlantic Cyclones, 1492–1996" (www.nhc.noaa.gov/pastdeadly.shtml), compiled by Edward N. Rappaport and Jose Fernandez-Partagas (28 May 1995). In "Appendix 1: Cyclones with 25+ deaths," number 119 is that of October 10–11, 1846, with 164+ deaths, while in "Appendix 2: Cyclones that may have 25+ deaths," number 422 is that of September 7–8, 1846, noting "several vessels lost offshore Virginia." The September hurricane remained offshore.

11 Junger, "Graveyard of the Atlantic."

12 Roads pp. 371–77.

13 Chadwick (1895) p. 624; Vickers (1994) pp. 286–87; Lord and Gamage p. 168. The 1850 census shows only 31 owners engaged in the codfishery in Marblehead (population 6,000), with 1 vessel each. The decline of the codfishery in Marblehead occurred gradually.

14 Morison (1921) p. 217.

15 Hazard (1969) pp. 73 and 210; Faler (1981) pp. 22–26.

16 "The stitching of the pieces that formed the upper part of the shoe required much the same skill that women used in making cloth and leather garments." Because of the regular losses of life due to fishing, Marblehead's population had more women than men (Faler pp. 25–26; Roads pp. 362–64).

17 Faler pp. 23, 58–60.

18 Roads pp. 358–64.

19 Hazard p. 43, n.1.

20 Johnson (1880).

21 One owner also took eight percent. of total receipts as "overhead." One captain took a much greater share than the other fishermen: ten percent. of proceeds after deduction of overhead and boat expenses, in addition to her share as crewmember. Greenlaw (1999), Appendix.

22 McFarland pp. 190–93.

23 Reynolds p. 167; Vickers (1994) pp. 278–79.

24 The average earnings of a cordwainer exceeded the average earnings of a fisherman, and were more predictable (Hazard p. 92, passim; Faler pp. 87 ff).

25 Chadwick (1874) p. 194.

26 "Various reasons are given for this abandonment of the fisheries. The increased expense and diminution of profits to owners, in consequence of modern methods; the absorption of the business by a neighboring port; the greater safety and more remunerative

employment offered to young men in the less hazardous calling of manufacturing, are each and all good and sufficient premises upon which to base sound conclusions.... No one regrets the passing away of the industry" (Roads p. 349–50; Vickers, 1994, p. 264). The suggestion by Bourne that the reason had to do with the railroad coming to Gloucester seems wrong, since it also came to Marblehead in 1839 (Bourne p. 87).

SIX

MARBLEHEAD'S FOREIGN TRADE AND SEA CAPTAINS, 1815–50

FISHING SCHOONERS WERE NOT THE ONLY VESSELS in Marblehead harbor. Marbleheaders also carried on an active foreign trade, both associated with fishing and otherwise. Schooners delivered cured fish to the West Indies and imported salt and other goods, though exports of fish to Europe declined to almost nothing by 1832 because of competition from British North America, and because of increasing United States markets for Marblehead fish.[1] But more diverse foreign trade was also carried on in larger, square-rigged vessels.

Marblehead shipowners employed 20–30 square riggers in foreign trade during the period 1815–40. The most prominent and wealthy shipowners after the War of 1812 continued to be the Hoopers (five descendants of "King" Robert Hooper were associated together) and the Broughtons. The Hoopers owned schooners and about ten square-rigged vessels in the 1820s, the largest of which were ships of about 300 tons and 100 feet in length—normal for the period. Nicholson Broughton's sons Nicholson, John, and Glover (two of whom married

Hoopers), and his grandson John Glover Broughton, were shipmasters and owners of schooners and about ten larger vessels.[2] These vessels carried cargos throughout the world, including Russia, South America, and the Far East. The names of the vessels, particularly the Hooper vessels, suggest some of their destinations: *Java*, *Ganges*, *Orient*, *Athens*, and *Pactolus* (a river that reaches the sea near Smyrna—now Izmir—in Turkey, on whose banks stood the ancient city of Sardis, capital of king Croesus).[3] These vessels paid large customs duties in Marblehead: the brig *Orient* paid between $13,000 and $17,000 in each of the years 1816–18 on cargoes from Calcutta, and $13,000 in 1820 on a cargo from Canton; and the ship *Java* (Nicholson Broughton, master) paid $39,000 in 1819 on a cargo from Canton.[4] The larger Marblehead vessels increasingly delivered their goods to Boston and other ports that had better access to markets than Marblehead.

Edmund Kimball also acquired ownership interests in square-rigged vessels for purposes of foreign trade during the latter part of this period: the ship *Maraposa* (110 feet, registered in Boston) in 1833, the ship *Nathaniel Hooper* (121 feet) in 1839, and the barque *Sardius* (96 feet) in 1843.[5] The *Nathaniel Hooper*, built in 1837 in Newbury for Nicholson Broughton and others, had in 1838 struck on Nantucket Shoal, been abandoned, found derelict at sea, and salvaged.[6] Edmund, along with Captain Francis Freeto of Marblehead, also had the barque *Mary Kimball* (116 feet) built in 1835 by Elias Jackman in Newbury and named for his first wife.[7] The *Salem Evening Mercury* for June 19, 1839, reported under "Disasters, Etc.":

> The Am. Consul at St. Helena [the island in the South Atlantic where Napoleon spent his last years] informed Capt. Macondry, of the ship *Ceylon*, at Boston, that barque *Mary Kimball* (of Marblehead) from Calcutta for Boston, (which put into Isle of France [Mauritius], dismasted and leaky) had been condemned.

But this was not the end of the *Mary Kimball*.

These vessels were engaged in a variety of foreign trade during the 1830s and 1840s. The *Maraposa* and the *Mary Kimball* went to India in 1835 and 1838, respectively.[8] The *Mary Kimball*, the *Nathaniel Hooper* and the *Sardius* went to Europe, the "cotton ports" (such as Charleston and New Orleans), and the River Plata (between Buenos Aires, Argentina, and Montevideo, Uruguay) during this period.[9] In 1841, Kimball contracted to carry emigrant passengers to the island of Jamaica on the *Mary Kimball*.[10] Shipowners could use brokers to arrange for cargoes in foreign ports, and could also advertise for cargoes through packet lines.

The packet lines were organizations featuring transportation of passengers as well as cargo between certain ports on a fixed schedule, sometimes called "square-riggers on schedule."[11]

Though potentially very profitable, foreign trade was complex and risky compared to fishing. Voyages to the Far East and back took a year or more, during which financial circumstances could change drastically. In 1835, Kimball and others sent the ship *Arno* (110 feet) to the Far East with specie (coin) and a letter of credit (a bank document guaranteeing payment of drafts or checks on certain conditions) to be invested in coffee or tea.[12] The letter of credit was drawn by Robert Hooper, Jr. at Boston (formerly of Marblehead), as agent for T. Wiggin and Co., London bankers. It authorized the master of the *Arno* to draw drafts (like checks, but not payable on demand) on Wiggin and Co. The master/supercargo found prices of coffee too high in Batavia, bought tin and rice instead, sold the rice in Canton, and loaded teas for home. He overdrew on the letter of credit in error, and the owners incurred a loss in the sale in Boston of the additional teas because of the financial panic of 1837.[13] The owners sued the master for this loss, and it was only in 1844 that the court finally decided that the master/supercargo, as the owner's agent (and not Russell & Co. in Canton), was responsible for the loss to the owner and shippers.

The *Arno* made another voyage to the Far East about a year later. The shippers obtained another letter of credit on Wiggin & Co. for merchandise to be purchased in Canton. Letters of credit were used in lieu of specie to avoid having to tie up cash for the long period of Far Eastern voyages. They generally provided for the drafts to be payable six months after sight (that is, six months after delivery of the drafts to Wiggin & Co. in London) to allow for the transportation of the goods purchased by the drafts to the United States and for the use of the proceeds of the sale of the goods to reimburse Wiggin & Co. before the drafts were payable.[14] The sellers of the goods in Canton would send the drafts to Wiggin & Co. in London for acceptance and later payment and would in effect finance the sale and bear the risk of nonpayment, subject to later recovery against the purchaser.[15] Drafts and other mail from the Far East was delivered overland to London by means of a British mail system through India, the Red Sea, the Mediterranean, and France. The delivery time at this period was about two months, much less than the four or five months needed for a ship to sail the approximately 15,000 nautical miles to London.[16]

Before the drafts drawn by Russell and Co. were due for payment, Wiggin and Co. failed during the financial panic of 1837.[17] To avoid dishonor of the drafts and the resulting impact on its business, Russell and Co. in Canton obtained payment of the drafts by another banker (Baring Bros.), but at a premium of 21 percent due to exchange-rate fluctuations in the meantime.[18] Russell and Co. sued the Boston purchaser of the goods to recover the excess premium, and the court (again, not until 1845) decided that Russell and Co., as the purchaser's agent, could recover this loss from the purchaser. Exchange rate fluctuations could be substantial over the long periods of voyages halfway around the world, and there was little that a merchant could do to guard against this risk, other than buy and sell only for coin, which would involve substantial costs and risks of its own.

As shipowners became specialized in carrying other shipper's goods "for freight" (the term used in the sense of "payment for shipping cargo"), they were subject to the same uninsurable risks of price fluctuations, nonpayment, and exchange-rate fluctuations with respect to the freight as the cargo owners were with respect to the cargo, but the risks of loss of the ship and cargo could be insured.[19] The *Boston Shipping List* for October 3 and 7, 1846, reported under "Disasters &c.":

> Scilly, Sept 8 – The Am ship *Mary Kimball*, Gregory, of and for Marblehead, from Cadiz, was abandoned 8th ult. [August], in lat 36N, lon 9W in a sinking state: crew picked up soon after by the Swedish bark *Valeria*, and since landed here by a pilot cutter.
> Bark *Mary Kimball*, abandoned at sea Aug 8, in lon 9, was valued at $18,000, and was insured at three offices in Boston, to the amount of $17,590.[20]

Not all Marbleheaders' voyages began and ended in the same port. As in fishing, Marblehead surpassed other towns in producing sea captains in foreign trade. Hundreds of Marblehead masters and skippers are listed in *Old Marblehead Sea Captains, and the Ships in which they Sailed*. Of these, the careers of about 150 extended after the War of 1812, and 20–30 were most active after that war.[21] Many of these men began their careers as young seamen on privateers during the War of 1812, and the rest began their careers either (like John D. Whidden and Josiah P. Creesy Jr.) in merchant vessels or (like Joseph W. Snow and John Bridgeo) in fishing schooners. Many, because codfishing was pervasive, skippered schooners at some point in their careers, between other commands or out of curiosity. Some of these captains owned and captained their own brigs in foreign trade; they answered to no sedentary owners, nor did they benefit from the aid of such owners when disaster struck.[22] Because of the limited number of local vessels involved in foreign trade, Marblehead captains increasingly looked outside Marblehead, primarily to Boston, for ships to command.

George Cloutman (1790-18__) was one whose career began in a privateer.

Lee Street today. Capt. John Girdler house, built 1821.

Beginning in 1826, he commanded the ship *Palladium* (103 feet), owned by Israel Thorndike (1755-1832), a prominent shipowner of Beverly and Boston. A log in the Marblehead Museum and Historical Society recounts her voyage to Sumatra and back in 1829-30. The log was kept by Samoht Yarb (Thomas Bray spelled backwards, 23 years old), a Marbleheader who apparently knew the Malay language, as the log is sprinkled with notations in the Arabic script (Jawi) then used by the Malays.[23] Upon reaching the west coast of Sumatra, the *Palladium* traded opium and drafts for coffee and pepper.[24] On June 3, 1830, at Tampa Juan (Tapaktuan) in Aceh in northwest Sumatra, Rajah Jeretoola

> confirmed that no Am vessel had loaded there this season. That there was plenty of pepper on shore. Ask'd $5 per picul. The Jeretoola also told us that about 15 days since an English brig was cut off at a small island call'd Eliz off ___ there were 12 lascars [East Indian sailors] on board the brig and they were murdered by about 30 [Acehnese] from a prow. This is excellent encouragement to begin with....[25]

LEE STREET.

From Drake's Nooks & Corners of the New England Coast

[June 4] offered pepper for $4 ¼ picul of 143 ¾ lbs....

[June 6] Rajah signed the contract 3 7/8 $ for pepper picul wgt 2400$. 2 lb allowance every draft....

[June 10] The Rajah's conduct appeared today entirely changed from what it has formerly been, he has always given us cocoa nuts to drink / which is a mark of friendship along the whole coast / to day he gave none; his behaviour in other respects was so equivocal, that as there were but about 20 bags of pepper round the scales, Capt. C. thought proper not to go ashore—We have taken on board not 1/3 of what they promised us, and there is no more in the place; there being no prospect of getting any more here, + the weather becoming bad, the season being so far advanced, Capt. C. concluded to go to Padang or Batavia after coffee —At midnight a light breeze springing up from the land, got up the anchor + got underweigh. About 1 am the two Jeretoola's came aboard + wanted to know why we went off without paying what we owed, the capt. stopped enough to pay for bags + mackerel they had / Capt. C. told them if they would produce the bags he would pay them, + would wait till the next day at 12 o'c. They accordingly sent their boat on shore + remained aboard the ship. At daylight 4 prows came out from Tampa tuan alongside the ship. There were from 30 to 40 malays on board. 3 had pepper + in the other was the Rajah + some of the head men—All the prows had arms conceal'd about them, the largest 2 long brass swiv-els, some muskets and swords—The Capt. allowed only the Rajah and 4 or 5 Malays to come on board, which frustrated any bad intentions they may have had. After some difficulty got rid of them—from the 3 boats took 210 bags pepper—A prow came alongside from Labon hadgic – said there was plenty of pepper at Labon hadgic, Muckei, Qualabattoo Alingin + Tallowpaw—wanted Capt. C. to go to Labon hadgic + load the ship—Bot some paddy + pumbkins from the Malays.

A year later, a Salem ship was attacked by the Malays at Quallah Battoo (Kuala Batu), and all the crew killed except the captain and a few men who were ashore. The next year, the U.S. Frigate *Potomac* was sent to avenge this and other attacks of the Malays, and demolished the Malay settlements.[26]

Lewis Russell (1793–1868), Lydia Kimball's half brother, began his career as a seaman on the privateer schooner *Industry* during the War of 1812, and became master of many ships. He lost two sons on his vessels in foreign ports from yellow fever, one at Port-au-Prince, Haiti, in 1842, and another in Sumatra in 1844. "Captain Russell was obliged to help cast both of his sons in the sea."[27] Lydia and Edmund could well sympathize with Captain Lewis: Edmund and Mary Kimball's son Thomas, who seems to have been interested in a seafaring life, "sailed from

New York as first officer of Brig *Martha* [on January 16, 1837] and was not heard from after."[28]

John Girdler (1805–53) commanded the *Nathaniel Hooper* from 1847 to 1852, and rescued the crew of a sinking British vessel at one point. His 17-year-old daughter Sarah Jane Girdler went on a voyage in 1857–58 on the ship *Robert H. Dixey* from Boston to Mobile, Alabama, and from thence across the Atlantic to St. Petersburg, Bordeaux, and finally back to Mobile, keeping a journal which was published in 1997.[29] She was a nanny to the baby of her aunt and uncle, Richard William Dixey (1809–60) of Marblehead, who commanded the *Dixey* in the cotton trade. Captain Dixey had commanded the clipper ship *Houqua* when it opened the Chinese port of Fuzhou to American trade in 1854.[30] He and 18 of his crew on the *Robert H. Dixey* went down in a hurricane in Mobile Bay in 1860.

John Girdler's brother Richard Girdler (1798–1865) commanded a "temperance ship"—one in which liquor was not allowed—from 1825–32, remarking:

> I sailed in the ship *Grecian*, upwards of two years, and had my shipping articles opened in large and legible characters, that no ardent spirits whatever should be allowed on board the ship…. I have lost no men by sickness or any other accident, and when visiting unhealthy climates, an early attention to the complaints of my crew has restored them to health. On the contrary, in pestilential climates, I have observed that intemperate seamen are generally victims, in consequence of their medicine having little or no effect on their constitutions.[31]

Another brother, Lewis Girdler (1793-1826), was murdered at Manila with his crew.[32]

Samuel Graves (b. 1804) crossed the Atlantic 78 times, and the Pacific 6 times. While captain of the barque *Elvira* in 1844, she was struck by the ship *Newark* in the fog, and the first mate and part of the crew jumped on board the Newark for safety. As later recalled by Captain Graves:

> Hard time. Set my broken leg myself, got up spars and sails to keep off shore, and was three days in a gale before getting into Philadelphia…. The other ship rendered me no assistance…. One of the hard times during 35 years at sea, collided three times, sunk one ship and a schooner, broke my leg and collar bone, taken and stabbed by pirates bound to Sumatra, relieved of twenty-two thousand Spanish dollars, returned home, other casualties too numerous to mention.[33]

George Henry Wilson (b. 1820) had his share of troubles. Under his command, the ship *Tonquin* ran aground on Whaleman's Spit ("afterwards known as

Tonquin Shoal") at the entrance to San Francisco Harbor in 1849; the clipper ship *Golden Racer* was stranded in the River Min (Fuzhou) and became a total loss; and the ship *Samoset* was lost at Fort Point, Golden Gate. But he continued to captain ships until 1870.[34]

Josiah Perkins Creesy Jr. (1814–71) is probably the best known of Marblehead sea captains, famed for his exploits in driving the clipper ship *Flying Cloud* (225 feet), built by Donald McKay in 1851, to San Francisco via Cape Horn in 89 days, not once but twice. Captain Arthur Clark says in *The Clipper Ship Era*:

> Like most boys who were brought up along the coast of Massachusetts Bay, he began his career by being skipper and all hands of a borrowed thirteen-foot dory, with the usual leg-o'-mutton sail, and steered by an oar over her lee gunwale.... [I]n this, during his summer vacation, he would make short cruises to Beverly and sometimes to the neighboring port of Salem.[35]

Josiah married Eleanor Prentiss of Marblehead in 1841, who had learned navigation from her father, Captain John Prentiss.[36] She acted as Josiah's partner by navigating the vessels they sailed in, including the *Flying Cloud*. After the *Flying Cloud*'s record voyage, Creesy and the ship were media stars. The ship's

> ...topmast fids [on which the topmast rested], crushed and broken, were taken up to the Astor House and exhibited to the admiration of the town [New York]. Her owners, Grinnell, Minturn & Co., had her log from New York to San Francisco printed in gold letters on white silk for distribution among their friends, and Captain Creesy fled to his home in Marblehead in order to escape notoriety.[37]

He later was appointed a commander in the U.S. Navy and assigned to the clipper ship *Ino*. She had a crew of 80 Marbleheaders and in 1862 made a record run of twelve days from New York to Cadiz.[38] Creesy's brother, William Andrew Creesy, was also a captain, and commanded the clipper ship *Mary Whittredge*, among other vessels.

John D. Whidden (1832–191_), whose *Ocean Life in the Old Sailing-Ship Days* (1908) is a charming and informative record of his career, was born in Boston, and moved to Marblehead to live with his grandparents, Thomas and Alice (Bray) Appleton, after becoming an orphan at age five. Against their wishes, he went to sea at age 12 in a merchant vessel. "To go to sea, become a sailor, visit foreign lands, and in due time become the captain of a fine ship, this was the goal to be looked forward to, the great aim of our lives."

His story is replete with his meetings throughout the world with other

Marblehead sea captains. In addition to those mentioned elsewhere in this narrative, he sailed with Captain Michael Gregory from New York to Boston in 1845; the pilot at Honolulu was Captain John Meek; Captain Hector Crowell Dixey was in San Francisco in 1850 with the schooner *Eagle* and William Swasey as mate. In 1851, at age 19, Whidden became third mate under Captain Knott Pedrick in the *Emperor*, engaged in the cotton trade. He relates how Captain Pedrick, with four hundred steerage passengers from Le Havre to New York, three-quarters of whom were women and girls of 17–37 years, invited the girls to dance on the poopdeck (a raised after-portion of the main deck). He allowed the crew to join them as partners, "and the kindness of Captain Pedrick was appreciated by all on board."[39]

In 1857, at age 25, Whidden got his first command, and continued to run into Marbleheaders. He rode horseback in Buenos Aires with Captain William Gregory; in 1858 he was first mate under Captain John Devereux on a voyage in which Horace Broughton was second mate, and John Bartol third. He described Captain Devereux as "the most genial of men, a good shipmaster of the old school." During an extremely cold and stormy winter approach to Boston, Devereux had ordered that a barrel of whisky in the cargo be broached and the crew given a drink each watch.[40] He officiated at the marriage of Captain Eben Graves in New Orleans in 1860; he employed Captain Knott P. Bray as captain of a vessel he partly owned, the *C.H. Jordan*; and in 1864 he met Captain William Swasey again, who by then was the master of a U.S. gunboat looking out for blockade runners in the Bahamas.[41]

Captain Whidden married twice, his first wife dying of cholera in Shanghai on her first voyage in 1862. His second wife enjoyed the sea life and learned to navigate the ship herself, like Josiah P. Creesy's wife.[42] "This was the most enjoyable period of my sea experience," he wrote, and argued strongly that captains should bring their wives to relieve the loneliness of command, and to act as a refining influence on the crews.[43] Finally, seeing that "[s]ince the close of the [Civil] war, the carrying trade had gone from bad to worse, and there was no money in it,"[44] he gave up the sea after 25 years. He does not recount a single incident that would qualify for reporting under "Disasters &c." in the daily newspaper, nor were any shoals or reefs named for any of his ships.

Francis Freeto (b. 1791) and John Bridgeo (1821–95; career described in chapter 9) were the Marblehead captains employed the longest by Edmund Kimball. Captain Freeto served in a privateer during the War of 1812 and skippered a schooner before becoming the captain of the ship *Maraposa* in 1833, the barque *Mary Kimball* in 1835, and the ship *Nathaniel Hooper* from 1839–47.[45] He was reputed to be worth $50,000 in 1850, and had the ship *Riga*, in which he owned a half share, built in Marblehead in 1856. He commanded her until she was sold in 1864 when he was 73 years old, after more than fifty years at sea. Although the life of shipmasters is often romanticized and glorified, several shipmasters' own accounts of their voyages often use the word "tedious" (or "teagous") to describe their voyages, but Freeto by contrast seems to have enjoyed himself.[46]

By 1840, the Hoopers had moved their base to Boston.[47] Robert Chamblett Hooper owned part of Union Wharf in Boston, on which his store was located, and the whole of Constitution Wharf.[48] Nicholson Broughton became bankrupt in 1842, and the Broughtons moved to Boston in 1845 or 1846.[49] But Edmund Kimball and others stayed in Marblehead, and undertook new ventures there. Kimball was 60 years old in 1846, and not ready to retire. His oldest son, Edmund Jr. (33 years old in 1846) was by then available to help in business. Edmund Sr. was still investing in new shipping, and in 1848 he had the Barque *Tyringham* (141 feet) built in Newbury. He still owned it as late as 1859. In one incident, the *New York Herald* for October 1, 1856, reported under "Miscellaneous and Disasters":

> Bark *Tyringham*, at Boston from Gefle [Gavle, a port 100 miles or more north of Stockholm, Sweden], on 4th and 5th inst., lat 53 lon 26, had a heavy gale from WSW to WNW, during which sprung fore and mainmast, sprung a leak, and threw overboard about 150 tons of iron. Is now leaking about 600 [tons] per hour.

Edmund and Lydia's youngest child, Anna Woodbury, was born in 1845, and his eldest daughter, Mary Knight, married Joseph Pitman Turner (a widower) on June 24, 1847. Kimball celebrated his success by having his and Lydia's portraits painted by William Bartoll, the leading portrait painter in Marblehead.

Endnotes

1   Morison (1921) p. 309. Ryan, p.84. Marblehead vessels brought salt from Cadiz into the 1840s.

2   "From 1825 to 1835 had built for [Nicholson Broughton] by Jackman and Currier of Newburyport thirty-two ships, brigantines and schooners many of them sailing from what is now [1915] the Marblehead Transportation Company's wharf, on foreign voyages" (Lindsey p. 24).

3   The *Salem Gazette* for April 17, 1838, reported under "Disasters Etc.:"

    Ship *Athens*, (of Marblehead) for Boston, sailed from Antwerp, Nov. 16, in ballast, and has not since been heard from. She was 15 years old, and insured at two offices in Boston for $8,000. Her roll of equipage when she left Boston, in Sept. contained the names of John E. Thaxter, of Boston, master; Joshua Otis of do. chief mate; Andrew Valentine, of Marblehead, second mate; and Wm. Fish, of Salem, one of the seamen.

4   Bradlee.

5   He also owned the barque *Wenham* (132 feet, registered in Newburyport) briefly in 1847.

6   *The Nathaniel Hooper*, 17 F. Cas. 1185 (Cir. Ct. D. Ma. 1839), Story, J. She was named for Nicholson Broughton's father-in-law, Hon. Nathaniel Hooper.

7   Cheney p. 74 ff. Two unlined pages of Edmund's account book contain an itemization of all the costs of this vessel, totaling $29,280.06. This comes to about $80 per register ton.

8   Marblehead Marine Ins. Co. records. The Phillips Library has a partial log of the *Maraposa*, Captain Gale, in 1835 for a voyage from Boston to Batavia. Microfilm 91, reels 30 and 39. The *Mary Kimball* is also recorded as arriving in Cape Breton and Liverpool in 1836, St. Croix in 1838, and Rotterdam in 1840. See www.cimorelli.com/cgi-bin/magellanscripts/.

9   Marblehead Marine Ins. Co. records. These three vessels also appear in the Marblehead port entry book and other records carrying salt, olives, raisins, leeches, hats and wine from Cadiz during the years 1837–47. Abstract of imports, and boarding officers record of arrivals, RG 036, 20/10/02–5 (National Archives and Records Administration, Waltham, MA).

10 *Richardson v. Churchill*, 59 Mass. 425 (Sup. Ct. MA. 1850).

11 Albion (1938), p. 14. They were prominent roughly from 1818 through the mid-1850s, when they began to be replaced by steamships. In 1851, there were 85 sailing

packet lines (including coastal lines) listed in New York, and by 1853, there were 50 transatlantic lines from a variety of east coast ports (Cutler, 1961, pp. 314–15). New York to Liverpool was the busiest transatlantic route, and the busiest coastal routes were New York to Charleston and New Orleans—the "cotton ports." Ships were sometimes associated part time with a packet line, or with more than one line, more for the purpose of advertising for cargoes for its owner than for charter to the packet line (Cutler, 1961, p. 249). The *Nathaniel Hooper* and the *Mary Kimball* were associated in 1844 with the New Line, running packet ships from Boston to Charleston, while in 1848 the *Nathaniel Hooper* was associated with Samuel Thompson's Line, sailing from New York to Liverpool, and in 1852 with the Eagle Line, running from New York to New Orleans.

12 The *Arno* was owned by Nathaniel Gould of Boston. General instructions were given to the master (who also in this case acted as supercargo in charge of the business of the voyage) as follows:

> ...to make all haste to Batavia [now Jakarta, Java], and there ... if practicable to load with coffee ... and return direct to Boston as soon as possible ... to purchase ... five hundred piculs of government Banca tin.... But if you cannot load for home at Java, please take a cargo of the best white rice you can find, and proceed to Lintin [near the mouth of the Canton River, about 60 miles below Canton]. Leave your ship there, and go up to Canton, and confer with Messrs. Russell and Company, and if you can load with teas prudently, you will please to put all my funds into their hands. Take the ship up to Wampoa [the anchorage for Canton, about 12 miles below Canton, where the foreign "factories," or warehouses, were based], and sell the rice.... [They] will send down some cassia in mats for you to take at Lintin, as you go up.... Should you find it impracticable or unsafe to load there, you can sell the rice at Lintin, and, as a last resort, go over to Manilla, and take a cargo of sugar and hemp.... Use bills [of exchange, or drafts] for the purchase of tin and rice at Batavia, and should you go to Canton, perhaps you may be able to negotiate your exchange at Batavia, to greater advantage than you can at Canton.... For funds ... fifteen thousand dollars (Mexican), $15,000, in specie, and a [letter of] credit for five thousand pounds sterling. You are to receive a commission of two and a half percent on all investments made at Java or Manilla, and two percent on those made at Canton.... In addition to your commission, I agree to pay you mate's wages, viz. thirty dollars per month, as master of the ship. (*Gould* v. *Rich*, 48 Mass 538, Sup. Ct. Mass. 1844).

13 In a letter to the master by the owner of the *Arno*, he referred to "the severe and successive losses I have sustained on that and subsequent voyages to Canton."

14 Hidy (1949) pp. 131, 136–37, and 140. Letters of credit were usually not secured by specific collateral.

15   "These bills [of exchange or drafts] were all payable in six months after sight, being the usual time on which bills, drawn in China on English bankers, were made payable, and they were sold by the [seller of the goods] in Canton, and went through India to England (as is the usual course of bills drawn in China) and were presented to and accepted by [Wiggin & Co.] in London" about six months after they were drawn. But acceptance is not payment; it is merely an agreement to pay in six months time (*Green* v. *Goddard*, 50 Mass. 212, Sup. Ct. MA. 1845).

16   Thomas Waghorn, a retired British naval officer residing in Calcutta "… was convinced that the Red Sea was the best route to India, and with government and commercial backing he began setting up the machinery of his line. His only land stages were those across France to Marseilles, and across a corner of Egypt from Alexandria to Suez [the Suez canal did not open until 1869].… In 1835 mail was conveyed by this route for the first time, and in the following year, 'by the indefatigable exertions of Lieutenant Waghorn,' letters traveled from London to Bombay in the astounding time of sixty days.… By July, 1841, he had succeeded in putting mail through from London to Bombay in thirty days and ten hours" (Harlow, 1928, pp. 197–98).

17   Wiggin and Co. was one of the British "three W's" which failed during this panic and subsequent depression (Hidy pp. 195, 217, and 222). The panic and suspension of payments in the United States extended from March to May, 1837 (Hidy p. 207).

18   As the court said, "The correspondents of the plaintiffs, in London, fortunately for them, were the house of Baring Brothers & Co., who had the strength to resist the current which swept away their neighbors." Baring Bros. was a British merchant banker with an American partner, and was prominent in financing American trade in this period. It emerged from the panic of 1837 as the preeminent house in this business (Hidy pp. 82, 123, 125, 127, and 234). Edmund Kimball used this house in his later shipping business. The premium on sterling, set by supply and demand at this time (before the gold standard and fixed exchange rates), rose from par (about 9 percent, according to the court) as financial conditions deteriorated (Hidy p. 145, 206–07).

19   Hutchins pp. 239–40. "Those maritime merchants who became wealthy lived dignified, sedentary lives while managing their fleets from their counting houses. The ownership of vessels staffed by his own masters and supercargoes, who could act independently and quickly abroad, try various markets, make advantageous contacts, and promptly relay information, was of the utmost importance to such an owner."

20   The bark *Sardius* was also "lost" in some way (Lindsey p. 94).

21   These included (along with any vessels of Edmund Kimball's they are known to have commanded): Knott P. Bray (*Nathaniel Hooper* 1847), John Bridgeo (*Marblehead*, *Mary*), Glover Broughton, George Cloutman, Josiah P. Creesy, Jr., John Devereux, Hector Cowell Dixey (*Compromise*, 1852), John Dixey (*Nathaniel Hooper*), Richard W.

Dixey, Ebenezer Evans (*Mariposa* 1834), Francis Freeto (*Mariposa* 1833, *Mary Kimball* 1835, *Nathaniel Hooper* 1839), William Blackler Gerry, John Girdler (*Nathaniel Hooper*), Samuel Graves, Michael B. Gregory (*Mary Kimball*), William Hammond, John Barker Lindsey, Richard Meek, Knott Pedrick, Lewis Russell, Samuel Tucker, John D. Whidden, George Henry Wilson. Abstract logs for many of Gerry's voyages (as well as his obituaries) are in the Phillips Library, microfilm 140, reel 14. He died in Calcutta of cholera on the maiden voyage of the clipper ship *Noonday*, which was built for him to command, and was buried in the Dissenters' Burial Ground there (he was a Unitarian).

22   These included: Benjamin Andrews (drowned near Sumatra in 1821), Phillip Bessom, John Conway, Asa Hooper, Richard Pedrick, Joseph Proctor Jr., John Proctor, John Quiner Jr., and Peter J. Rogers (Bradlee, Lindsey).

23   Bray's father, Edmund, and brothers, John and Knott Pedrick, were sea captains.

24   For example, May 9 (Padang): "Sold to a boat from shore a case of opium;" July 9 (Batavia): "Sent on shore 2 cases opium."

25   Aceh at this time was generally independent of Dutch or British control. En.wikipedia.org/wiki/Aceh .

26   See www.sabrizain.demon.co.uk/malaya/potomac.htm and "Voyage of the United States Frigate *Potomac*" Jeremiah N. Reynolds, New York: Harper and Brothers, 1835.

27   *Salem Evening News*, 1937–38, microfilm scrap book, Abbott Public Library, Marblehead. Russell left many logbooks which have not been found. As examples of the interrelations among Marbleheaders, Lydia Kimball was also related to other sea captains during this period: John Girdler, Knott P. Bray (b. 1802), who commanded the Nathaniel Hooper in 1847, Richard Evans (b. 1799), and William Hammond (b. 1797). Lindsey p. 56. See www.girdler.com/girdline.htm.

28   Family Bible in the author's possession. The *Martha* (95 feet) was owned by Nathaniel Cunningham of Boston and others, and sailed to Appalachicola, Florida. *Boston Daily Atlas*, January 20, 1837.

29   L. Tracy Girdler (1997). The *Robert H. Dixey* (185 feet) was built in 1854 in East Boston, and was partly owned by the eponymous brother of Captain Richard Dixey. She is not usually included in lists of clipper ships, but was built for the cotton trade.

30   Howe and Matthews p. 276.

31   Letter quoted in "Temperance," p. 501. By 1834, most of the merchant ships sailing out of Boston and New York did not permit ardent spirits for the crew (pp. 502–03). The same was true for whaling ships sailing out of New Bedford, but only 27 out of 77 whaling ships from Nantucket were temperance ships, and it appears that fishing

schooners also still used ardent spirits. Insurance companies encouraged temperance by discounting insurance for such ships (Whipple, 1987, pp. 271–72).

32 Lindsey, p. 57; VRM.

33 Lindsey pp. 62–64; Roads pp. 328–30.

34 Lindsey p. 132; Howe & Matthews. His journal for the *Tonquin* on October 16, 1847, reports: "P.M. torrents of rain, came near being boarded by a waterspout – fired the starb. gun & dispersed it" (Phillips Library, 656, 1847/49T).

35 Arthur H. Clark (1910) pp. 153–54.

36 Binney (1852) p. 139 indicates that Eleanor (born 1814) was the daughter of Captain Joshua Prentiss III (1790–1817) who died at Havana. Her mother Eleanor (Horton) Prentiss then remarried, to Joshua's brother John (1792–1840), who was a lieutenant in the U.S. Navy (VRM).

37 Arthur H. Clark p. 211.

38 *Ibid.* p. 253.

39 Whidden pp. 100–01.

40 Ibid., pp. 165, 168, 169–70.

41 Captain Swasey received $10,000 as his share of prize money over a period of six months.

42 Whipple (1987) pp. 84–85, 109, and 144; Shaw pp. 45–47.

43 Whidden pp. 287–89.

44 Ibid., p. 308.

45 He married Elizabeth Crowninshield in 1817 and they had a daughter, Mary Jane (VRM).

46 Daggett (1988) pp. 19, 36, and passim.; Sandwith Drinker (1990) pp. 57–58; Morison (1921) p. 358, quoting Matthew Fontaine Maury; log of the ship *Charlotte*, Wm. B. Gerry, for December 19, 1843.

47 Morison (1921) p. 217. Forbes and Greene, an estimate of the wealth of residents of Massachusetts in 1850, list only two Hoopers in Marblehead: John Hooper ($1,500,000), President of the Marblehead Bank, Director of the Eastern Railroad, and interested in cotton manufacturing; and John Hooper's sister, Mrs. William Reed ($200,000). The third wealthiest in Marblehead was Edmund Kimball ($150,000).

48 Lindsey p. 81.

49 *Knott P. Bray* v. *John D. Bates*, 50 MA 237 (Sup. Ct. MA 1845), a suit by Knott P. Bray of Marblehead, master of the barque Mary Broughton, for recovery of wages.

SEVEN

SHIPBUILDING IN MARBLEHEAD, 1849–52

UNTIL 1847, SHIPBUILDING IN MARBLEHEAD apparently had been limited to a few schooners and other small vessels, and little even of that in the later years. There was, however, a considerable amount of repair work carried out in the town.[1] In 1847, Edmund Kimball and others organized a new shipyard:

> The place selected for the building of Mr. Kimball's new ship is an excellent spot....It is known as Red Stone Cove, on account of the reddish appearance of the rocks in that vicinity. It opens to the harbor on the south, where the water is of a sufficient depth at a short distance from the shore to float a frigate, and on the other side is encircled by high hills, which slope gradually to the water. In the cove or enclosure, there is sufficient room for three large ships to be on the stocks at one time. The Planing Mill is in immediate proximity, and the Rope Walk but a short distance off, while the Essex Railroad which is arranged so as to connect with the Marblehead Branch, by which the best of timber can be brought direct from the interior to this town, make the selected spot an excellent location for the permanent establishment of a shipyard.[2]

A schooner was built at this shipyard in 1847 for local owners, and in 1849 the first full rigged ship, the *Robert Hooper* (155 feet), was built there for Edmund Kimball.

This shipbuilding enterprise represented a large organizational effort, and an unusual one in that it built the largest vessels for only one shipowner, Kimball himself. The shipyard used land owned by Henry F. Pitman (a wealthy trader and landowner in Marblehead), and in 1854 Kimball, Pitman, and Joseph Pitman Turner (probably a relative of Pitman's) bought some adjacent land.[3] Kimball built homes for the shipyard workers, and there were also sail lofts in town.[4] As the principal promoter of the shipyard, Kimball arranged for master carpenters to come to Marblehead to carry out the construction, and probably bore most of the financial risk with respect to the seven full-rigged ships built for him.[5] But Pitman and Turner also supported the shipyard: they were each one-third owners with Kimball of the clipper ship *Mary*, one-third owners with Knott Martin II of the schooner *Ariel*, half owners of the schooner *John Phillips*, and Pitman was part owner of two other schooners built there. During a ten year period, the shipyard built eight ships, a brig, and 19 schooners for Marblehead owners (see Appendix D). The schooners were "clipper built," not the bluff bowed vessels of earlier days.[6]

The building of these ships coincided with a tremendous national boom in shipbuilding between 1847 and 1857. One of the major spurs driving this boom was the discovery of gold in California in 1848. Ships built during this period were on average three times as large as those that had been built before, and reflected advances in models, rigs, and techniques of construction. "In nearly every town whose waterway could float a large ship the construction of freighters or clippers was undertaken. In some of these no such large vessels had been built before." The shipbuilding business did not require more than "a graded launching place and a set of bed logs and ways." It was highly competitive, and "few fortunes were made in shipbuilding comparable to those achieved in commerce."[7]

The critical element of any ship construction was the master carpenter. The master carpenter of the *Robert Hooper* is not known, but the next two, and the last, ships were attributed to "Henry Ewell master carpenter."[8] The intervening three ships, all clippers, were built by Benjamin Dutton (1813–84), who also built several ships on the Merrimack (and in Virginia) from 1849 to 1863, including the clipper ship *Victory* (1857) in his home town of Newburyport, and who later built ships in Boston.[9] As a type, the master carpenter

Benjamin Dutton, 1813-1884, master carpenter.

was a man of many accomplishments, for he was usually responsible for the design of the ship, the selection of the timber, the details of construction, the organization of the work in the yard, and the launching of the vessel.... Owners normally allowed builders a wide amount of discretion in design, only the general features of vessels being given in the building contracts, and, accordingly, each master fashioned his model according to his notions, which were largely based on observations and experience.... Builders took into consideration in their work the wishes of the owners, the admeasurement rules, the nature of the trade in which the ship was to be employed, and the requirements of speed and carrying capacity. There was little scientific information available....[10]

At the beginning of the 19th century the hours of work were from sunrise to sunset, but later these were reduced to a 10-hour day, six days a week. Grog (rum and water) was commonly served at 11 a.m. and 4 p.m. Construction of a fully rigged ship took less than a year. The ships were built of white oak with pine coverings, fastened with iron and copper, and had two decks with a half poop.[11] They were generally rated "A1-" (considered "First Class,") when new for insurance purposes.[12] The ships would be based in Boston and New York, because after 1850 the only foreign trade coming to Marblehead was schooners bringing wood and coal.[13]

The *Robert Hooper*

A fine ship of 700 tons [155 feet], belonging to Edmund Kimball, Esq., is to be launched from the ship yard in Marblehead, next week…. We trust that this is only the commencement of a new and profitable business for our industrious neighbors. The timber for this vessel was brought over the Essex Railroad [opened in 1839], and we are informed that the enterprise has proved quite satisfactory to those engaged in it, as showing that vessels can be built more cheaply in Marblehead than in any place the builders had before worked in.[14]

The launching, which took place on the 31st of October [1849], was witnessed by hundreds of people, many of whom came from the neighboring cities and towns. Business was generally suspended, and the day was observed as a holiday throughout the town. The enterprise thus begun, for a time gave promise of becoming one of the permanent industries of the town. Six other ships of from eight hundred to twelve hundred tons burden were subsequently built for Mr. Kimball; and within a period of nine years twenty schooners of from eighty-seven to one hundred and twelve tons burden were built for various persons engaged in the fishing business.[15]

The *Robert Hooper* was likely named for "King" Robert Hooper or his descendants. "'King' Hooper had promoted the export of fish by Marbleheaders and had become rich in the 1740s and 1750s. He was nicknamed 'King' for his integrity and fairness to his fishermen."[16] William Churchill, master mariner from New York City, was 1/4 owner and captain of this ship, as he had been of the *Nathaniel Hooper*, the *Tyringham*, and the *Mary Kimball*, and would be of later ships built in Marblehead.

The gold rush proceeded apace. As early as January of 1850, 62 Marbleheaders had gone to California on 23 different vessels, seven as captains, and another nine had gone by way of the Isthmus of Panama.[17] Edmund Kimball Jr. moved to New York in about 1850 to act as ship's agent, sometimes called ship's husband, to arrange for cargoes, repairs, and legal matters such as clearing at the custom house. In early 1850, the *Robert Hooper* made her first voyage to Liverpool, and, in September of that year she was in New York, advertising for a voyage to San Francisco. A Charles Zellweger paid $250 for the 16,000 mile five-month passage to San Francisco by way of Cape Horn on the *Robert Hooper*, but when the ship's departure was delayed because of a storm, he decided to go via the Isthmus of Panama, presumably in haste to get to the gold fields, and brought suit to get his money back.[18] The judge gave him half his passage money, as Edmund Jr. had previously offered.[19] The ship left New York under Captain Pike on November 7, carrying eight passengers, and arrived April 11, 1851, a passage of 153 days.[20] The *Hooper* was not a clipper, and 153 days was about average for the voyage.[21]

In 1853, to raise funds for larger ships, Kimball sold the *Hooper* to Augustus Zerega of New York, who had packet lines to Liverpool, Antwerp, and Glasgow.[22] The *Boston Shipping List* for May 13, 1854, included the following notice: "Ship *Robert Hooper*, Spencer, sld from Liverpool Feb 21, for New York, has not since been heard from. She was an old ship formerly of Marblehead." In fact, she was only four years old.[23]

The *Compromise*

The new shipyard gave the Marblehead newspaper some bragging rights in the town's rivalry with Salem:

> We learn that the keel for a ship of one thousand tons burthen has arrived in town and will be laid at the shipyard of E. Kimball, Esq. in a few days. We write this sign of increasing prosperity for the especial edification of our neighbor of the *Salem Register*.[24]

> The new ship is a splendid model of marine architecture, and one which will do infinite credit to the enterprising gentleman who conceived and carried into execution the design of ship building in Marblehead. No sooner was the business established and regarded as a successful operation, than our nearest neighbor, Salem, made an ineffectual attempt to keep pace with the times, by considering the expediency of establishing a ship yard in that city.... They are erecting a miniature ship, and the wise men of that city will be called upon in the course of time, to consider how to propel her into her destined element; that there will not be sufficient depth of water to float her is amply proven by the large number of vessels that have stuck in the mud of that harbor.[25]

> The new ship will be launched on next Tuesday, the 3rd of December [1850]. Her length, by Government measure is 158 feet 4 inches, breadth 33 feet, and depth 16 feet 6 inches. The name designed her is (Freetrader), and is 794 ton burden. We hope the weather will be favorable.[26]

> The new ship was launched on Thursday at 1 o'clock. The weather was extremely favorable for saving slush on the ways, the rain falling in sufficient quantity to keep them well wet; notwithstanding which a large number of people assembled at an early hour to witness the interesting spectacle. She went off in grand style, and was immediately taken in tow by the steamer *R.B. Forbes* and sailed to Boston. Just before going

Bird's Eye View of Marblehead by J.O.J. Frost, circa 1920. Courtesy of Marblehead Museum and Historical Society

to press we learned that none of the names given by the community generally suiting the proprietor, a compromise was effected and she was named the *Compromise*.[27]

Kimball was 3/4 owner of the *Compromise*, with the remaining 1/4 share being owned by the ship's captain, John Riley, of Dover, NH. She began her career with a voyage to Liverpool with the Red Z line of packets (Augustus Zerega, master). Liverpool was the principal British port for American ships, being at least a day closer than London, and centrally located for industry as well as emigration, which increased greatly during this period.[28] In 1853, the *Compromise* was sold to Zerega.

The *Anna Kimball*

In February 1852, about a year after the launch of the *Compromise*, the *Anna Kimball* (161 feet) was launched in Marblehead, named for Edmund and Lydia's youngest daughter, who was then six years old.[29] According to a painting in the 1920s by Marblehead artist J.O.J. Frost (1852-1928), which is shown, Frost's sister was named after this ship.[30] Although the Marblehead ships at times were regular traders between certain ports when cargoes were available, much of the time they were "transient ships," sometimes called "tramp ships," particularly in their later years. This would be especially true of the career of the *Anna Kimball*.

> The transient picked up cargoes wherever they might be found, carried them wherever business directed at the moment and might thus knock around from port to port for a year or more without visiting the same one twice.[31]

Or, as Melville's Redburn says, "they are here to-day, and somewhere else tomorrow, like Mullin's dog."[32] A later captain and part owner of the *Anna Kimball*, Charles Marsh, would describe her as follows in a deposition: "The ship is rather a dull sailer, especially in light winds; in strong breezes and fair winds we get along with a middling class of vessels." However, Kimball would own her for longer than any of his other ships.

The *Anna Kimball* made a maiden voyage to Liverpool, and then went to San Francisco with 28 passengers and on to Calcutta with Edmund Kimball's son William as third mate, a generally unnecessary position sometimes used for owners' representatives.[33] Edmund regularly sent his sons on voyages as junior officers to gain experience. John had been a seaman on the bark *Tyringham* in 1849, and Edmund Jr. would also go to sea.[34] An item under "Disasters &c" in the *Boston Shipping List* for April 15, 1854, reads:

> Ship *Anna Kimball*, of Newburyport [sic], (which put into Portsmouth E[ngland] after contact with bark *Bonita*, of Liverpool, which was sunk), had her stem split, and wood-ends started.

"Contact" was the usual term for a collision, which in this case was clearly an understatement from the point of view of the *Bonita*. An item in the *New York Tribune* under "Disasters &c" for June 20, 1856 reads:

> Ship *Anna Kimball*, from [Manila] for this port, which put into Singapore 7th March in distress, having completed repairs, sailed again 9th April. The repairs cost about $6,000.[35]

As the shipbuilding and shipping business in Marblehead proceeded apace, Edmund Kimball began in 1853 to shift his principal residence to Wenham, his hometown some 10 miles inland from Marblehead.[36] He did this despite having lived in Marblehead with his family for 46 years, having married into two locally prominent families, and having made his fortune there.[37] In a letter to his daughter

Mary dated July 1, 1852, he gave her a mortgage for her son, Edmund Kimball Turner, then four years old, saying that

> perhaps it will be well for you to let this amount accumulate for ten or twelve years at which time the principal and interest will amount to two thousand dollars. At that time (if the boy should live) he will be old enough to go out of town to school, and the yearly interest of this sum would pay his expenses and put him through college, and after he gets through college he would have the principal to set him up in business of some kind. He may buy a small farm with the money and turn his attention to agriculture. I have always thought that a person with a good education on a farm makes the best citizen that we have in this country. A man with a good education generally has considerable influence in the town where he resides, and being on a farm he has considerable leisure to get information.... I have made the above suggestions but you can do with the money as you please.... P.S. Say nothing.[38]

But Mary died later the same year, on November 4, 1852.[39]

After a lifetime of industry and excitement as a shipowner, Kimball thinks the best life for his grandson (and namesake) would be that of an educated farmer. Even after moving to Wenham, however, he continued to direct and control his shipping business, probably from offices in Marblehead. Unlike most shipowners, Edmund never had a partner to assist him and share the risk in the shipping business, except for Turner's and Pitman's involvement with the shipyard, and with the ship *Mary*.[40] He never made his son Edmund Jr. a full partner or a part owner of any of his ships.[41] Despite Wenham's proximity to Marblehead, and the connection between them (and with Boston and New York beyond) by train and telegraph, it appears that Kimball lost contact with the shipping business as time went on.[42] He continued to build ships while the shipping business was deteriorating and others were cutting back. He probably was excited about his plans to build larger, faster ships, and may also have felt some responsibility for the shipyard he had promoted.

ENDNOTES

1   The first ship recorded as having been built in Marblehead was the *Desire*, built in 1636 (Roads p. 485). Only two schooners were both built and registered in Marblehead between the Revolution and 1847: the *Good Intent* in 1813 and the *Talus* in 1838. See Appendix D.

2   "Strolls About Town," *People's Advocate and Marblehead Mercury*, February 17, 1849. The cove is now nearly filled with a large stone wharf (built in 1894) on which sits a power plant, with the Marblehead Yacht Club at its base. A public park is located on the end of the wharf. Red Stone Lane is nearby.

3   Salem Registry of Deeds, book 500, pp. 81–83 (1854). Henry Florence Pitman was baptized in 1809, the son of Thomas and Elizabeth; he married twice and had several daughters. Joseph Pitman Turner was baptized in 1803, the son of Samuel Turner and Sarah Pitman of Salem (1793–1847). He married (first) Ellen Andrews, who died in 1846, and (second) Mary Kimball in 1847 (VRM).

4   Lord and Gamage p. 301. The shipyard is not mentioned in the 1850 U.S. Census, although a "Cordage Co." is (National Archives, Waltham, MA, 1850 Census, microfilm T1204, manufacturing, Barnstable-Middlesex counties, roll 5). The Cordage Co. had 30 employees and a value of $126,000. The owners are not listed. *The Massachusetts Register and Business Directory* for 1852, by George Adams, lists for Marblehead: three sailmakers (Thomas Gilbert, Elizur Graves, and Samuel Lyon); the Essex Cordage Co.; a carpenter (Benjamin Dutton); and two shipbuilders, Edward (sic) Ewell and James Topham. Kimball had bought a sawmill in Orono, Maine, in 1837, which probably supplied much of the lumber.

5   The Edmund Kimball of Marblehead papers in the Phillips Library include a series of 100 drafts drawn by Henry T. Ewell on Edmund in 1850–52 totaling $3,025, apparently for the construction of the *Anna Kimball*. It seems likely that the ships were built on a time and materials basis, rather than on a fixed-price basis, with Edmund supplying some of the lumber.

6   *People's Advocate and Marblehead Mercury*, May 22, 1852, and December 24, 1853. Three of the schooners were built at a shipyard in Second Cove, near Quiner's wharf, according to the shipyard file at the Marblehead Museum and Historical Society: the *Amy Knight*, the *Boys*, and the *Helen*.

7   Hutchins pp. 105, 103, and 273-5.

8   Ewell was a resident of Newbury (Salem Registry of Deeds, book 382, p. 97). He and his wife Mary had a daughter, Caroline Brooks (Newbury Vital Records), and a son, Henry, when they were living in Marblehead.

9 Cheney, pp. 128–29; Salem Registry, book 373, p. 290; Cutler (1930) p. 418. He married (first) Martha Ann Ash, and they had six children; he later married Harriet Small (*The Dutton Family of Newburyport*, Mass., http://rad.duttonfamily.com).

10 Hutchins pp. 109–16.

11 *American Lloyds Register*, which began publication in 1859, and the *New York Marine Register*, which was published in 1857–58, published classification lists of American vessels, together with details of ownership, construction and repairs (www.mysticseaport.org/library/initiative/MsList.cfm). Apart from these sources, ownership information is difficult to find for vessels registered in New York and other ports where registry abstracts are not readily available. The *List of American Flag Merchant Vessels Receiving Certificates of Registry in the Port of New York*, (National Archives, 1968) does not list owners. The author has obtained from the National Archives copies of certificates of registry in New York for the *Wenham, Tyringham, Robert Hooper, Compromise, Belle of the Sea*, and *Lady Washington*.

12 "The degrees of 1st and 2nd class will imply confidence for the transportation of perishable cargoes on long voyages" (*American Lloyds*, 1859, p. 16). "When built of White Oak, in frames, and pine coverings, copper butt and wood end bolted, treenailed through and seamed on the ceiling, and all other fastenings first class, will class A1-, denoting that the character is not quite equal to first class" (p. 23).

13 Bradlee p. 101.

14 *Salem Register*, October 15, 1849.

15 Roads pp. 270–71.

16 Roads p. 500; Bowden p. 125. Another Robert Hooper owned many vessels in Marblehead in the 1820s and died in 1843. Account book p. 156. The latter Robert Hooper's will was litigated in *Robert Hooper, Executor* v. *Henry Hooper & others*, 63 MA 122 (Sup. Ct. MA, 1851). See also chapter 6 re *Gould* v. *Rich*.

17 *People's Advocate and Marblehead Mercury*, January 19, 1850.

18 Voyages to California from the east coast, considered coastal trade after the annexation of California in 1846 during the Mexican War, were restricted by law to vessels built and owned in the United States (Navigation Act of 1817, 3 U.S. Stat. 351; Hutchins pp. 252 and 266). "775 vessels cleared from eastern ports for California in 1849, and several hundred departed annually during the next eight years" (Hutchins p. 266).

19 *Zellweger* v. *The Robert Cooper* [sic], 30 F. Cas. 918 (D.C.S.D.N.Y. 1852).

20 Maritime Heritage.

21 Cutler (1930) p. 153. As noted in chapter 6, the clipper *Flying Cloud* made it in a record 89 days, while some ships took over 200. The *Mary* would make it in 112 days in 1857, and the *Belle of the Sea* in 128 days on her maiden voyage in 1857, and in 134

days in 1860. Cutler, 1930, pp. 508 and 519. Howe and Matthews contains histories of the *Elizabeth Kimball*, the *Mary*, and the *Belle of the Sea*, but (like other secondary sources) has some errors which are corrected herein.

22 Howe and Matthews p. 488; Cutler (1961) p. 308.

23 Disappearance of ships without a trace was not unusual. In a survey of vessel disasters between 1847 and 1850 based on Lloyd's of London records, 204 out of 12,041, or 1 out of 60, losses were unexplained (Wreckage).

24 *People's Advocate and Marblehead Messenger*, February 2, 1850.

25 *People's Advocate and Marblehead Messenger*, November 9, 1850.

26 *People's Advocate and Marblehead Messenger*, November 30, 1850. Only occasional copies of Salem and Marblehead papers have been found.

27 *People's Advocate and Marblehead Messenger*, December 7, 1850.

28 In 1851, with James Riley listed as master, the ship was associated with the Black Star Line, running packets from New York to Liverpool. Britain had repealed her corn laws in 1846 and her navigation laws in 1849, so American vessels could compete on equal terms in foreign trade. Before 1847, emigration rarely exceeded 100,000 per year, but in 1849 and 1850 it jumped to almost 300,000, and in 1854 it exceeded 425,000.

"Liverpool… had certain advantages over London as a port for American trade. It was a day's sail nearer in point of distance, and usually several day's sail nearer in time, owing to delays commonly incident to working up and down the English Channel. Its central location with regard to Great Britain and Ireland made it a convenient point of embarkation for emigrants…. The situation of Liverpool with respect to the mines and heavy industries … was of still greater importance. With few exceptions, all the nation's coal, salt, lead, and iron mines were concentrated within a hundred miles of the city's docks. The same was true of all the heavy manufactures … cottons and woolens." (Cutler, 1961, pp. 101 and 317).

29 Annie died on October 6, 1865 at the age of 20, according to the family Bible in the author's possession.

30 Frost began painting in 1922 at age 70 to preserve what he knew of Marblehead history. He could not sell his paintings, but is now considered an important native artist and his paintings hang in many American museums. "JOJ Frost" by Gail Pike Hercher, Marblehead Magazine, at legendinc.com/Pages/MarbleheadNet/MM/Articles/JOJFrost.html. Painting courtesy of Marblehead Museum and Historical Society.

31 Albion, 1938, p. 15.

32 Melville chapter 23.

33 On January 11, 1853, it was reported in San Francisco that the *Anna Kimball* was expected to arrive with 28 named passengers (Maritime Heritage Society). The *Anna Kimball* then headed for Calcutta. The Shipping Articles for this voyage (the official agreement between master and crew), dated May 11, 1853, show a planned voyage to Calcutta, India, then on to a port in Europe before sailing home (having circumnavigated the globe). Samuel B. Pike is captain, and William P. Kimball (then 23 years old) third mate. There were two other mates, a steward, cook, two boys, and 14 seamen, all in their 20s, of whom eight are from east coast ports and six from European ports. About 16 seamen was the normal complement for these ships.

34 Letter from John to his sister Lydia, dated September 27, 1909.

35 Further repairs were made in October, 1856. Other than for early 1854 and 1856–57, no comprehensive survey of the disaster reports has been made by the author.

36 He bought two acres on Main St. in 1852, and another acre in 1854. "In or about 1852 [Edmund] built a large house and barn and other buildings in Wenham near the Hamilton line on the north side of the highway on land that formerly belonged to the 'Gardner Farm' (Capt. John)." "Index to Homesteads in Wenham by Wellington Pool," Wenham Historical Society. This house is at the corner of Main St. and Linden St. on the Hamilton border. The Wenham Museum has photographs of this house in 1894 and 1904.

37 In Forbes and Greene, Edmund's "commonly reputed" worth was given as $150,000, with the statement: "Began with limited means. Was first a carpenter, then went into the fishing business, and is now a ship-owner" (p. 73). Edmund is listed as the third-richest man in Marblehead, after two descendants of "King" Hooper. Also listed, at $50,000 each, are Francis Freeto and William Hammond, who had captained Edmund's ships. The Dun & Co. report for November 15, 1854, states that he was worth $200,000, and was an "A No. 1" credit risk (Massachusetts, vol. 21, p. 182, R.G. Dun & Co. Collection, Baker Library, Harvard Business School).

38 In the Turner family file at the Marblehead Museum and Historical Society. Mary had married Joseph P. Turner in 1847, a widower who became cashier of the Grand Bank. They had Edmund's first grandchild, Edmund Kimball Turner, on May 11, 1848, and a daughter, Mary Ellen Turner, on October 25, 1851, who died at age 4 months, before the letter was written. Edmund K. Turner graduated from the Massachusetts Institute of Technology in 1870.

39 Joseph Turner continued as cashier for 37 years, until 1874, when he was succeeded by his son by his first marriage (*Marblehead Messenger*). He owned interests in schooners, as well as the *Mary* (Bradlee).

40 "Most of the New York [shipping] concerns took the form of partnerships" (Albion, 1939, p. 263).

41 The Dun & Co. report on Edmund Jr. for May 1855 states, "Ae 55 marr'd is from
    Mass and came to this city over 10 years ago and com'd the shipping bus at 106 Wall
    St. under the firm of K & Shelton, was afterwards of K & Hale and since their diss'n
    some years ago has done a com bus on his own a/c ... and to the transaction of his
    father's bus in this city." (New York, vol. 344, p. 465, R.G. Dun & Co. Collection,
    Baker Library, Harvard Business School).

42 Karr (1995) pp. 255–63; Standage (1998) p. 128.

EIGHT

Shipbuilding Continues, 1853–57

T HE MARBLEHEAD SHIPYARD HAD HIT ITS STRIDE, and in the nearly two years between the launch of the *Anna Kimball* and the *Elizabeth Kimball*, it produced ten clipper-built schooners. The next ships would include three clipper ships built by Benjamin Dutton. The term "clipper ship" defines a set of characteristics that emphasized speed over capacity.[1] The *Elizabeth Kimball, Mary*, and *Belle of the Sea* were "medium" clippers, "fine, sharp, fast ships, but cleverly designed to carry very heavy cargoes."[2] The year 1853 marked the peak of the California clipper traffic and clipper ship construction.

The *Elizabeth Kimball*

The *Elizabeth Kimball* (169 feet), named for Edmund and Lydia's second-youngest daughter Lizzie, was launched in December 1853.[3] She had a deck cabin for passengers, and "was considered to be a fast sailer under ordinary conditions."[4] She began life with European voyages.

John D. Whidden of Marblehead joined the *Elizabeth Kimball* as first officer for a voyage from Boston to Calcutta, with a cargo of ice, in 1855. He describes the ship as "a fine large ship of between eleven and twelve hundred tons, half clipper."[5]

> At this time, the ice business with the far east was a great trade. Ice was carried out at a low rate of freight, preferably to the ship's going in ballast, and bringing high prices when retailed from the ice-houses, it became a complete monopoly and paid big profits.[6]

Upon arrival off the mouth of the Hoogly River, one of the channels through which the River Ganges flows into the Bay of Bengal, they took a pilot for the five-day, hundred-mile sail upriver to Calcutta, then the British capital of India.[7]

> The pilots are a most skilful class of men in the management of a ship, having to serve a long apprenticeship as leadsman, second mate pilot, mate pilot, and finally master pilot, their term of service to master pilot covering some twenty years, during which time it is necessary to make two voyages to England, to become perfectly conversant with the workings of a ship. What they did not know about the working of a ship in a tideway, or swift current, was not worth knowing. From the moment they stepped on board, followed by their leadsman and servants, their orders were law....
>
> Going into moorings in the inner tier to discharge our ice, a bridge of boats was made, with a plank walk about four feet wide, from the bank to the ship, the ice blocks being hoisted from the hold and lowered over the ship's side upon the heads of three coolies stationed to receive them. It was very hot, and the moment the cold ice water began to trickle down their black backs, they would shiver, and strike a bee line for the ice-house, never stopping until their load was off their heads. During the discharging, our ship was a popular resort for all the officers of the surrounding ships, and iced drinks were concocted in every shape. Barrels of apples that were buried in sawdust in the hold were found when opened at the ice-house to be in good condition, the apples readily bringing from fifty to seventy-five cents each. While the ice lasted, we had no end of visitors....
>
> The spirit of caste is strong, and the contrast between the wealthy class and the masses, who suffer the most abject poverty, is very sharply drawn and painfully evident.... Hindooism forced itself upon the attention against the strong background of English prejudice and customs, and bodies were cremated at the burning ghauts, while the ashes and partly burned remains were thrown into the river as of old. It was a common thing in the morning to clear away four or five corpses from the ship's gangway....

Having taken on a cargo of jute, saltpeter, and other products of India, in due course our lading was completed, and the ship unmoored, and hauled into the stream in charge of the harbor pilot....

One night, when off the southern end of Ceylon, we were sailing with a smooth sea and an eight-knot breeze, the moon being near its full, and about four bells in the midwatch, while sitting on the weather side watching the ship's progress, and admiring the beauty of the night, the ship suddenly seemed to stop, the sails that had been rounded out asleep flapped violently, back and forth, and there was rumbling sound that seemed to proceed from the hold, with a trembling throughout, as though the keel was dragging across a reef. For a moment I was startled, thinking we had struck a shoal, but an instant's reflection convinced me there were no shoals in that vicinity, and it flashed upon my mind that we had experienced a submarine earthquake, and a severe shock at that. Captain Freeman rushed on deck, as well as the watch, but finding no cause for alarm, again went below.

Taking the S.E. trades fresh, the course was shaped for the south end of Madagascar, when the ship sprung a leak that made lively work at the pumps. The heavy seas in the Bay of Bengal, against which the ship had been driven, had started the wood ends about the water-line, causing the oakum to work out, developing a leak which grew worse daily until it took two thousand strokes per hour to keep her free.[8] As the leak was known to be just below the water-line, alongside the stem, Captain Freeman decided to touch at Mauritius, an island in the Indian Ocean about five hundred miles east of Madagascar, and without entering Port Louis, come to anchor in smooth water just outside the port, when, by shifting everything aft, bringing the leak out of the water, it could be got at and stopped. This was successfully accomplished. Raising the island in the forenoon, we ran in for the port, and dropped anchor in smooth water.

Rolling all water casks aft, bringing the stem out so the carpenter could get to work, before night the leak was stopped, and gave us no more trouble during the homeward voyage. It was a good piece of work....

Having passed the Bermudas and the Gulf Stream, we struck soundings, heading for the South Channel between Georges Banks and Cape Cod.

Favoring winds, but foggy weather, prevailing, we were bowling along about eight bells in the last dog-watch, when the ship struck on the south shoal of the island of Nantucket, with a force that startled all hands.

"Hard up!" came the order, and the *Elizabeth Kimball* responded. She never fully stopped, but dragging through the sand, paid off, and in a few moments was clear from the shoal, having just scraped its outer edge, and sustained no serious damage. The fog prevented our seeing anything. It was a narrow squeak, but in this case, "a miss was as good as a mile."

Rounding Cape Cod Light the following morning, and taking a pilot on board, passing Boston Light and the islands of the harbor, we let go our anchor one hundred and twenty-two days from Calcutta.

On Whidden's next voyage, also to Calcutta with ice, on the *Brutus*, Captain Meacom of Beverly, Edmund Kimball Jr. was second mate.

The *Mary*

A year after the *Elizabeth Kimball*, the *Mary* (179 feet) was launched in December 1854, fully rigged, ballasted and ready for sea. Kimball, Joseph Pitman Turner, and Henry Pitman each owned 1/3. Kimball's daughter Mary, who was also Turner's wife, had died two years before.

Three paintings of the *Mary* are shown. The first, a very nice painting by William York, a Canadian-born artist, made in 1859 for her captain, John Bridgeo of Marblehead, shows the *Mary* in heavy weather, under reefed topsails and a storm jib, with the foretopsail blown out and the men working to control it.[9] The second is an undated "owner's profile portrait" by an unknown artist.[10] The third shows the *Mary* just before launch in Red Stone Cove, with the red stone in the foreground.[11] The paintings, together with the two paintings of the *Belle of the Sea* below, present an interesting contrast. "Owner's profile portraits" were the most common type of ship painting.

The owner had worries enough. Why should he hang over his mantel a view of his ship on her beam ends in a squall? Such views were more commonly commissioned by captains, but the owner wanted an exact profile, yards braced well up with all plain sail drawing, full and by.[12]

In the York painting, the *Mary* is not depicted with skysail yards, which the *Elizabeth Kimball* and the *Belle of the Sea* had, and is shown with traditional single topsails, rather than the double topsails shown on the *Belle*'s paintings. These differences may be a result of the time of painting, or the limited information available to the artist. Only the York painting is known to be a contemporary work.

The flow of clipper ships had begun to ebb. Nearly half the total number of clippers built had been launched during 1853.[13]

Clipper Ship Mary *by William York, 1859. Courtesy of Richard Bridgeo.*

Clipper Ship Mary *by unknown artist. © Mystic Seaport, Mystic, CT*

Clipper Ship Mary *prior to launch, fully rigged.*

In the five years from 1851 to 1855 inclusive, the country had launched nearly 2,500,000 tons of the finest craft afloat, a scant 500,000 tons less than its entire fleet in 1850.[14]

Stagnation became pronounced in the shipping business during the summer [of 1854]. September saw New York harbor and wharves crowded with waiting vessels, 777 ships in all, including many clippers of the largest size. Similar conditions prevailed in Boston. All the time the shipyards were turning out new vessels.[15]

Despite these conditions, the *Mary*, captain William Churchill, sailed to New Orleans and Havre (the port of Paris, at the mouth of the River Seine) with cotton, and then from New York to San Francisco in 152 days in 1855–56.

The *Southern Belle*

Edmund launched the *Southern Belle* (183 feet) in March 1856, a little more than a year after the *Mary*. He owned 7/8, and Captain Christopher Lewis of West Yarmouth, MA, owned 1/8.[16] The origin of the name is unknown.[17] Her maiden voyage was from Boston to Liverpool and return. However, the *Boston Shipping List* for November 8, 1856, reported:

> Ship *Southern Belle*, (of Beverly), Lewis, from Liverpool for Boston was spoken Oct 16 lat 44 03 lon 50 03 by the [bark] *N Boynton*, from Marseilles. The next day at noon the ship was discovered to be on fire. The crew secured what provisions they could and went on board the bark. At 8 pm the flames broke out in a mass. The bark lay by her until midnight, and at 3 am the flames suddenly disappeared. The Southern Belle, 1,198 tons, built at Marblehead this year, and valued at $60,000. She had a valuable assorted cargo, a portion of which is insured in New York, and the balance in Boston.[18]

Joseph W. Snow Jr. of Marblehead (whose uncle Samuel Snow had gone down with all hands in the schooner *Splendid* in 1831) was mate. "The ship caught fire on the Grand Banks, which landed him in New York with nothing but what he had on."[19] No information on the cause of the fire has been found, but Kimball apparently did not blame Captain Lewis or Snow, as they became the captain and mate respectively of the *Belle of the Sea* a few months later. This loss must have been a blow to Edmund's confidence, if not a substantial financial blow.[20]

A Lloyd's of London survey for the years 1847–50 shows all the disasters occurring to vessels insured by Lloyd's, primarily British vessels of all sizes, as follows.[21] Similar proportions probably applied to American vessels.

> Driven on shore by stress of weather, in fogs, parted from anchors &c., vessels damaged but got off again. Cargoes partially or totally lost: 5,117
>
> Collision, at sea, or in rivers, vessels compelled to be run into port in a sinking state: 2,665
>
> Wrecked: 2,295
>
> Sailed and never heard of again: 204
>
> Abandoned at sea, water-logged, dismasted, on fire, crew taking to boats &c: 679
>
> Foundered at sea in consequence of collision, capsizing, leakage, swamping, &c: 883
>
> Burnt by accident: 87

Blown up: 7 by coal dust; 1 by spontaneous combustion; 4 by gas; 1 by
    powder (total 13)
Burnt by cargoes igniting: 11 coals; 1 flax; 1 wool; 3 cotton (total 16)
Damaged by ice: 51
Struck by lightning: 15
Plundered by pirates, and destroyed: 13
Taken possession of by convicts, and wrecked: 1
Struck by a whale and abandoned by crew: 1
Struck by a waterspout: 1
Total: 12,041

There was no Bethel for ships to go to when old, and as long as they
could be insured (or even if not) they sailed on, often to a disastrous end.[22]
Appendix F is a random example of the "Disasters &c" column of the *Boston
Shipping List* (September 26, 1857).[23] Ships today are vastly different, but
the sea has not changed. *Lloyd's List* for December 18, 2003, reports under
"Casualty Report":

> *Dina K* (North Korea) London, Dec 16 – Following notice to mari-
> ners broadcast at 1310, UTC, Dec 15: Distress signal received from gen-
> eral cargo *Dina K* (2092 gt, built 1971) in lat 36 00N, long 35 42E. *Vessels
> in vicinity requested to keep a sharp lookout, assist if possible. Reports
> to Larnaca RCC. London, Dec 16 – Following received from Larnaca
> RCC, timed 1450, UTC: Only a liferaft was found from general cargo
> *Dina K*. Search and rescue being conducted by Coast Guard Turkey as
> the vessel was in their area. London, Dec 16 – Following received from
> Coast Guard Ankara, timed 1500 UTC: General Cargo *Dina K*: One
> empty liferaft found, no other wreckage sighted. An aircraft conducted a
> search yesterday and today and nothing found so far.

The *Riga*

The *Riga* (140 feet) was launched on December 12, 1856. It was owned
equally by its captain, Francis Freeto, and William Courtiss, both of Marblehead.[24]
Captain Freeto (65 years old) was reputed to be worth $50,000 in 1850, and risked
much of it in the *Riga*. The *Salem Register* for February 26, 1857, had:

> Ship *Riga* at New Orleans for Boston, reports Jan. 20 in heavy gale,
> had bowsprit carried away just inside the cap; at 2 p.m., cut away the
> fore topmast which carried away the head of the foremast and main royal
> mast just above the eyes of the top gallant rigging. Had to cut everything

adrift, there being a heavy sea running, it being dangerous to keep them alongside for fear of staving a hole in the ship.[25]

She then left for Liverpool, and continued sailing primarily back and forth to Europe.

The *Belle of the Sea*

[In 1856] not a few ships that had been driven at top speed to California, Melbourne or China lay at their destinations for weeks, only to be forced to sail for other ports with all or a considerable part of their original cargo intact. Many of those fortunate enough to dispose of their merchandise found it almost impossible to secure profitable charters, and drifted into the wretched coolie or guano trade.[26]

The story of the clipper ship is the record of a losing fight. The significant fact is that after two or three years of the most intense and

Clipper Ship Belle of the Sea, *by C.S. Raleigh, 1892. © Mystic Seaport, Mystic, CT.*

Clipper Ship Belle of the Sea, *by unknown artist.*

colorful competition the world had seen, the youth of the land tacitly abandoned the field for no other reason than that life had become easier, more interesting and more profitable elsewhere. Men who were too old to change or had no wish to do so, carried on. The era was closed by the men, for the most part, who saw it begin, and not by a new generation of smart young sailors.[27]

The *Belle of the Sea* (188 feet), launched in early 1857 (a year after the *Southern Belle*), was the largest, no doubt the most expensive, and the fastest clipper built in Marblehead.

Launched - At Marblehead 23rd Inst [of February], a first class clipper ship of 1,255½ tons, called the *Belle of the Sea*. She was built by Ewell &

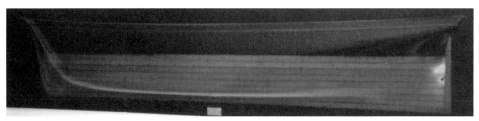

Half model of Belle of the Sea

> Dutton for Edmund Kimball, of Wenham, and will be commanded by
> Capt. Christopher Lewis. Has since ar' at Boston.[28]

But she would not be able to get underway immediately:

> In 1857 a ship measuring 1,000 tons, owned and built by Edward
> Kimball [sic] of Marblehead, was launched, and on the way down to
> deep water she broke through her cradle, spread the ways and landed
> on a ledge suffering great damage. Nothing was said about loss of life or
> injury to the launching crew who were frequently under the vessel cut-
> ting out keel blocks when she launched.[29]

The ship apparently was towed to Charlestown for repairs, where there was a
marine railway, and was subsequently relaunched in April.

The large half model of the *Belle of the Sea* shows the characteristics of a typical
medium clipper: a "straight" stem, vertical sternpost, gently sweeping sheerlines
(rail higher at the bow), minimal deadrise (rather flat bottom), moderate tumble-
home (inward curve of side above waterline), moderately sharp bow flared outward
to the deck, somewhat concave bow below waterline, and small counter (underside
of overhang at stern).[30]

Copies of paintings of the *Belle of the Sea* by Charles Sidney Raleigh in 1892
(long after she was lost), and by an unknown artist, are shown.[31] The *Belle of the Sea*
was supposed to be a crowning achievement, but it was not a propitious moment.[32]
The clipper ship bubble was about to burst.[33]

ENDNOTES

1   Crothers (1997) pp. xi, xv; Hutchins pp. 294–95.

2   Cutler (1930) p. 321; Howe and Matthews pp. vi–vii.

3   Lizzie died June 4, 1859, at age 17, according to the family Bible. This and later ships had a hailing port (the port of origin painted on their stern) of Beverly, Massachusetts, which was the closest port to Wenham, where Kimball then resided. Letter from Edmund Jr. to brother Charles, dated December 6, 1883.

4   *New York Marine Register*, 1858; Howe and Matthews.

5   The following extracts are taken from Whidden pp. 124–31.

6   The shipment of ice to the far east, as well as to the West Indies and the southern states, was pioneered by Frederick Tudor of Boston (1783–1864). He began in 1805, initially losing money and being pursued by creditors for twenty years, but eventually he became wealthy. Ice was originally cut from Fresh Pond in Cambridge, Massachusetts, and later from other lakes and rivers, including Wenham Lake in Wenham. It was stored in icehouses in sawdust insulation, and shipped from Charlestown. Apples were first shipped with the ice in 1816, and ice was first sent to India in 1833 (Weightman, 2003, p. 126). All that was required during the voyage was to pump out the meltwater and keep the hatches closed. The British colony at Calcutta built an icehouse to store the ice, and ships sailed right up to it. When ice was harvested from Walden Pond in Concord, Henry David Thoreau wrote, "Thus it appears, that the sweltering inhabitants of Charleston and New Orleans, of Madras and Bombay and Calcutta, drink at my well." (*Walden*, 1854, chapter 16). In 1847, 95 ships sailed with ice to foreign ports, but Calcutta shipments remained the most profitable.

7   Calcutta had been founded in 1690 by the British East India Company, a private company that held a monopoly on British trade with the East Indies from 1600–1813, and a more limited monopoly on British trade with China from 1813–34. MacGregor, p. 9. The British government took over the administration of its Indian empire in 1858, after a rebellion by Indian troops against the harsh rule of the Company. American trade with Calcutta had begun in 1784. Albion (1939), p. 204.

8   The ends of the bottom planks against the stem of the ship had sprung out somewhat.

9   Howe and Matthews p. 388; see also Lindsey p. 17. This painting, recently cleaned, is in the possession of Richard Bridgeo, great-grandson of John Bridgeo, her captain, who probably had it painted after he took command in 1857. It is signed "Wm York 1859, Dor." William Gay York (sometimes spelled Yorke) was born in Canada and later moved to England. He had a son, William Howard York, who also was a marine

painter. Mr. Richard Bridgeo, himself an oil tanker captain for many years, recounts a story of Captain Bridgeo's young daughter Anna (1846–95), on one of the *Mary*'s voyages to Mobile, sitting on a keg of gunpowder intended for Union soldiers so that her skirts would hide it from the Southern inspectors.

10 Brewington (*Marine Paintings*) no. 536. It includes a house flag of a white circle on a blue ground. If Kimball had a house flag, it has not been identified.

11 A humble effort by the author.

12 Laing (1971) p. 260.

13 Cutler (1930) p. 280.

14 Cutler (1961) p. 316.

15 Cutler (1930) pp. 290 and 308. In 1855, the brig *Curlew* (116 feet), owned by Samuel Hooper, was built in Marblehead.

16 Captain Lewis had been master of the *Elizabeth Kimball*.

17 The author has an unfounded suspicion that Edmund Jr.'s wife was from the South.

18 The *New York Herald* for October 31, 1856 (p. 8) under "Arrived" reported: "Bark *N. Boynton* (of Thomaston), Hosmer, Marseille, Aug 30, Gibraltar, Sept 16, with mdse, to Dutilh & Co. Oct.... 16th lat 44 03 lon 50 03 spoke ship *Southern Belle*, from Liverpool for Boston; 17th at 12 m saw a ship to windward running for us; at 1 pm spoke her, she proved to be the *Southern Belle* on fire. The captain requested us to lay by him until the condition of the ship could be ascertained; on opening the hatches the ship was full of smoke and on fire; got out what provisions they could, and came on board the *N Boynton*; at 8 pm the fire broke out in full; lay be her until midnight, and then left her burning; at 3 am 18th the flames disappeared suddenly;... The *NB* has experienced heavy NW and westerly gales the whole passage, split sails, etc." The *Boston Daily Atlas* reported the loss on October 31 and November 1, 1856, and in addition on November 10, 1856, reported: "A burning ship, about 1,000 tons, having a female figure head, painted white, apparently clipper built, and new, was fallen in with no date lat 43.26 lon 52.07 by Brig *Prince George* at St. John N.B. (probably the *Southern Belle* of Marblehead from Liverpool for Boston before reported burned at sea)." The position places the ship about 1,000 miles east of Nova Scotia.

19 Lindsey pp. 115–16. Later, Snow (1829–1911) was master of several ships, and in 1870 took charge of the Baker Island guano operations in the Pacific for a year, where "he came near being murdered by the natives, getting information in season from one of them, to enable him to escape."

20 The Dun & Co. credit report for Edmund for December 3, 1856, states, "lost a ship recently, but insured, credit not affected." (Massachusetts, vol. 21, p. 182, R.G. Dun & Co. Collection, Baker Library, Harvard Business School.)

21 Wreckage pp. 175–76.

22 Some were converted to barges or storage hulks, some were burned as a simple way of reclaiming their metal content, and some simply rotted (Crothers p. 492).

23 This column was published 2-3 times a week in the *Boston Shipping List*, a four-page newspaper devoted to shipping news. The paper also tracked arrivals, clearances, and speakings of American ships throughout the world, and contained market information, advertisements, and other maritime information. Newspapers of general circulation, such as the *New York Herald*, also contained this information.

24 William Courtiss of Boston married Mehitable Appleton of Marblehead in 1839 (VRM). Her brother Thomas Appleton would later have an interest in the ship. They were uncles and aunt of Captain John Whidden. Curtis was listed as owner in 1861 and 1862 (*American Lloyds*).

25 Lindsey pp. 53–54.

26 Cutler (1930) p. 320.

27 *Ibid.* p. 310.

28 *Boston Daily Advertiser*, February 28, 1857. Apparently, no records of Christopher Lewis have survived (Kittredge, 1935, p. 252).

29 Cheney, p. 357.

30 Crothers pp. 32–56, fig. 3.1 type 2. The half model is made of 13 layers of wood, with intervening thin strips of different color wood. It could be disassembled to take the measurements of the ship at various points during construction. The scale of the model is about 1/3" to 1', larger than the normal ¼" to 1'. The concave bow below the waterline enhanced speed, whereas the convex bow above the waterline reduced plunging into seas and permitted workspace on the foredeck. The small counter reduced impact of following seas. The model is in the author's possession.

31 The copy of the Raleigh painting is from the Mystic Seaport Museum, Mystic, CN (Mystic # 1974.928). The copy of the other painting is in the author's possession. The latter painting was owned in 1944 by Mrs. Penelope Sears Platt of Kingsport, Tennessee, who stated in a letter to Charles H. Kimball II, "As I understand it, my great grandfather Captain Nickerson was a part owner of the ship, and my grandfather, Captain Joseph Henry Sears had this painting." Raleigh (1830–1925) was born in England, went to sea, and was a self-taught artist who became a decorator, house painter and marine artist in New Bedford, and after 1881 in Monument Beach, Massachusetts (Brewington, *Dictionary*, p. 316).

32 Edmund was registered as 7/8 owner and Captain Christopher Lewis as 1/8 owner. The Dun & Co. report for July 16, 1857, states that Edmund is "still successful in bus. And wealthy, though his ships are not earning as much as formerly." (Massachusetts,

vol. 21, p. 182, R. G. Dun & Co. Collection, Baker Library, Harvard Business School).

33 The 1857 panic and crash in financial markets was preceded by what is usually described as a speculative bubble in railroads and wheat, but the speculation in clipper ship construction was just as pronounced (Kindleberger, 1978, pp. 16–19, 37, 115 and 129). Although the clipper speculation was primarily on a wholesale level among shipowners, "[t]he enormous cost of construction caused Boston shipowners to finance clippers by the public sale of stock," as in the railroads. *Boston Looks Seaward*, p. 132. Shares in ships could be purchased for as little as $1000. Albion (1939), p. 268.

NINE

SHIPPING DECLINE: CAPTAIN JOHN BRIDGEO

ALTHOUGH MANY SHIPBUILDERS AND OWNERS had experienced the long boom of the later 1840s and early 1850s, and began to cut back as freights declined after 1853, few apparently predicted the severity or duration of the panic and depression that finally came in 1857–58. Banks began to fail in August 1857, a general suspension of payment followed, and eventually thousands of businesses failed. Freights, which had been $40 per ton, fell to $10 per ton—the level they had been in the early part of the century.[1]

> The depression, first apparent in 1853, which had been growing more pronounced with each succeeding year, culminated during the autumn [of 1857] in a world wide financial debacle of unprecedented fury, which swept away thousands of firms and left the business world in a gloom which lasted for several years.[2]

> January of 1858 was the darkest within the memory of the oldest merchants, both at home and abroad. From England word came back that British shipping was facing its worst depression in history. There and in America hundreds of the finest craft afloat were accumulating in

their home ports. New York reported 800 or more, all of the larger sort, many of which were laid up for periods ranging from six months to two years.[3]

In a certain material sense the clipper ship era ended in 1857. No new clippers were launched thereafter…. A scant half dozen racers were launched in '57.[4]

No one has successfully estimated the amount of red ink which went into the ledgers of those shipowners who turned out too many of these glorious swift craft [after the first few clipper owners had skimmed the cream of the Pacific trade].[5]

In addition to the general business decline, the events that had conspired in the early 1850s to stimulate shipping, and therefore shipbuilding, reversed themselves. The California trade declined, emigration declined, the foreign (mostly British) demand for American shipping declined, steam replaced sail on the packet lines, and these stimulants were not replaced with any new demand for shipping. The only substantial trade that continued for a while was the shipping of cotton. The immediate impact of this depression on Marblehead shipping was to put the shipyard out of business. It also changed a generally profitable shipping business to a marginally profitable or largely unprofitable one that left little margin for error or accident.

The *Anna Kimball*'s Voyage to Melbourne and Calcutta

Before the panic, on July 4, 1856, Kimball hired out the *Anna Kimball* on charter to a firm of the Lyman family for a voyage from New York to Melbourne, Calcutta and Boston for $35,750, or about $42 per ton.[6] This charter fee probably represented more than half the cost of constructing the ship, and would allow Kimball a large profit even after the deduction of expenses, which included the wages of the master and crew under the charter.[7] But it was a long way to Australia, India, and back, and only a portion of the charter fee was paid up front.

The captain was Thornton B. Rennell, and his wife accompanied him. After leaving Calcutta the ship had heavy weather and leaked badly. They put into the British island of Mauritius in the Indian Ocean for repairs, one of the few places on the sailing track from the Far East where a captain could have substantial repairs made. On October 6, while the ship was undergoing repairs, and without knowing what was going on there, Kimball agreed to sell a "master's interest," or 1/12 of the ship, to Rennell for $4,000, which assumed a $48,000 value for the ship. In Mauritius, the crew, who had shipped at Calcutta, complained to the master of ill treatment by the mates, and of want of provisions (especially beer). Rennell did not investigate the complaints, but had the crew put in jail ashore for 33 days. When the crew came aboard again, there was a confrontation between them and the captain, other captains in the port, and the police, during which shots were fired. Shortly before the ship arrived home, the charterers became bankrupt without having paid the balance of the charter fee. Out of this troublesome voyage, three separate lawsuits arose and wended their weary way through the courts over the following years.

In the first case, some of the crew brought suit against the master under the Boston Federal court's Admiralty jurisdiction because of his treatment of them. The "humane" Judge Peleg Sprague (1793-1880) held that the master had a duty to investigate the crew's complaints, because the mate could not lawfully inflict punishment on his own, and that Rennell had been unjustifiably rash and precipitate in jailing and confronting the crew.[8] He stated:

> I am sorry to say, that the refusal of the captain to listen to the seamen, is not extraordinary; on the contrary, from the numerous cases which have come before me, I am induced to believe, that it is the course usually adopted by ship-masters.... Masters, also, too often shirk the responsibility that belongs to them, respecting the discipline of the crew, and throw it upon the mates, who have no right by law to inflict punishment.... [A] ship's company is a little community by itself. Its head, or governor, is invested with large powers, and is bound to extend his protection to all its members, and they ought not only to receive, but, as far as practicable, to be convinced that they will receive, equal justice at his hands, whatever their respective stations or duties.

He awarded damages totaling $860.00 to the crew. It is questionable whether the crew ever recovered the sum, as they tried to claim it from funds owing to Rennell in the hands of others, including Kimball, but he disputed owing money to the master. He was finally discharged as garnishee without liability in 1862.[9]

In the second case, Rennell sued Kimball, claiming that Kimball refused to pay him what he was owed. Kimball's contract with Rennell, whose part ownership of the vessel had not yet taken effect, provided that Rennell would be paid five percent of the gross earnings of the ship, rather than a salary—a common arrangement. It is not clear how this case was resolved, as the reported decision required that a special judge consider additional evidence.[10] When the ship was registered again in 1858, Charles Marsh of Newburyport is recorded as the master, and owned a 3/24 interest. Rennell still owned his 1/12. It is not known where

Kimball found Rennell to be captain of the *Anna Kimball,* or where he found the other shipmasters from outside Marblehead that he employed. The Marblehead shipmasters he employed, and whose careers are mentioned herein, had a more sympathetic attitude toward their crews than Rennell, and did not get themselves into the kind of trouble that Rennell had with his crew.

In the third case, Edmund brought a "libel" in Admiralty to assert a lien on the failed charterers' cargo for the unpaid balance of the charter fee, over $10,000. Kimball's suit was opposed by other creditors of the Lymans with an interest in the cargo, but the Lymans supported Kimball's version of the facts.[11] Richard Henry Dana, Jr. unsuccessfully argued the case for Kimball in the trial court; it was finally determined in Kimball's favor by the U.S. Supreme Court in December 1865, eight years after he had expected to be paid.[12] Litigation at this time was inexpensive, and maritime litigation was particularly common, but a final resolution of disputes was often more protracted even than today.

Richard Henry Dana Jr. (1815–82) had achieved fame early for his *Two Years Before the Mast* (1840), the story of his voyage as a seaman aboard the brig Pilgrim from Boston to California in 1834.[13] He began his career as a trial lawyer by representing seamen against captains and mates, because of his experience under the sadistic Captain Thompson of the Pilgrim. By the time of the *Anna Kimball* case (1859), he had for years been handling more lucrative business cases, like Kimball's, and "his forensic reputation then stood at its height."[14]

In one of Dana's earlier cases, when he represented seamen, he obtained a judgment by Judge Peleg Sprague against a master because he disciplined a seaman for complaining about the wanton severity of the mate, much like the Rennell case, and because the master failed to permit the crewmember to complain before the American consul in a foreign port, as required by an 1840 Massachusetts statute.[15] In another case, Dana obtained a judgment by Sprague for wages for the crew even though no freight (the earnings for shipping cargo) was earned on the voyage because the ship was wrecked. The normal Admiralty rule was that "freight is the mother of wages," and no wages at all would be owed to the crew for a voyage if freight was not earned by safe delivery of the cargo.[16] As Sprague said: "That maxim is probably indebted to the concise figure of speech in which it is conveyed, for something of its force and acceptance." In this case, the ship *Massasoit,* on a voyage from Calcutta to Boston, went ashore in a December storm at the mouth of Boston harbor. The crew barely escaped with their lives, and were physically unable to perform any labor while agents of the owner attempted to save parts of the wreck. Sprague stated:

That policy which makes the compensation of the seamen depend on his saving property, entrusted to his care, for the owner, was intended to secure his fidelity, and stimulate his exertions in case of disasters, which usually occur at sea, or in remote countries, where the owners cannot be present.... Surely the stern rule of maritime policy, which has been adopted to stimulate continued exertions for the benefit of the owner, has no application to a case like this; and the just principles which usually govern contracts for labor need not be intercepted.[17]

The *Belle of the Sea*'s Voyage from London to Melbourne

In contrast to the *Anna Kimball*, the *Belle of the Sea* was a long-distance runner. On her maiden voyage in 1857, the Belle went to San Francisco (126 days, with "light winds and calms for 38 days to port") and then around the world via Calcutta and London.[18] She then made a passage from London to Melbourne, reported by Captain Arthur H. Clark in his *Clipper Ship Era* as being made in a record 64 days.[19] This record is repeated by subsequent authors, but Howe and Matthews note that "no dates or other confirmatory evidence is now obtainable."[20] However, the *Boston Shipping List* has the *Belle* clearing London on September 7, off Portland Bill on September 15, and arriving at Melbourne on December 18, 1858, far in excess of 64 days. A search of the Melbourne newspapers shows that the *Belle* did arrive about December 18 with a miscellaneous cargo (no passengers, mostly ardent spirits), and the official Melbourne port records confirm this, so the Arthur Clark report is an error.[21] In connection with another record reported by Clark, Morison speaks of "the untrustworthiness of second-hand and subsequent statements of sailing ship's records."[22]

Kimball's strategy, during this time of financial stress, was to keep his ships moving, even at greatly reduced freights and thin or nonexistent profits. Whether this was a better strategy than laying the ships up, as the famous *Flying Cloud* was for two and a half years, and as many others were, is difficult to say.[23]

The *Mary*'s Voyage to San Francisco and Calcutta

Under the right captain, the *Mary* could also be a long-distance ship. She found such a captain in John Bridgeo of Marblehead, the son of skipper Philip Bridgeo. He became, after Francis Freeto, the second-longest-serving captain of a Marblehead ship (1857–64). John left school at 13 in 1834 to sail on the schooner

Clipper ship cards courtesy of Peabody Essex Museum, Salem, Massachusetts.

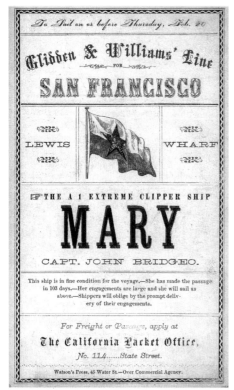 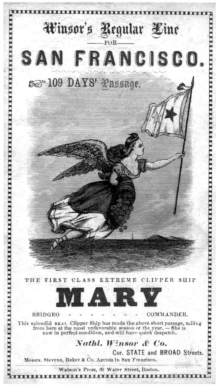

Clipper ship cards courtesy of Peabody Essex Museum, Salem, Massachusetts.

William, and was skipper of the schooner *Marblehead* at 22. He was a mate in the *Mary* from the time she was launched.[24]

His first voyage as captain was from Boston to San Francisco, Calcutta, London, Cadiz, and home.[25] The passage to San Francisco was made in the very fast time of 109 or 112 days, though its log has not been found.[26] Of 630 clipper ship passages to San Francisco from Boston and New York in the years 1852–57, only 68 were made in 109 days or better.[27] The California clipper trade was all about speed. Fast clipper ship passages were used by brokers and owners to advertise for cargo on subsequent voyages, as shown by the clipper ship sailing cards for the *Mary* and the *Belle of the Sea*. The *Mary* is called an "extreme" clipper on both cards, and on one card a passage of 103 days is claimed. The *Mary*'s 109-day passage is said to be in the "unfavorable season," as it was against the strong prevailing westerlies in winter in the Southern Ocean. One of the *Belle of the Sea* cards also lists a 103-day passage, which can only refer to her reverse passage to New York from San Francisco in 1861 (with the prevailing westerlies around Cape Horn), when she made the coast of New York in 103 days but then had contrary gales for three days. Such hyperbole was common, especially when cargoes were scarce. It was not necessary in those days to state that past performance does not guarantee future results.

The *Mary*'s Voyages from New Orleans to Havre

The Mary made a series of voyages in 1859–61 between New Orleans (or Mobile, Alabama) and Havre, France, or Liverpool, carrying cotton.[28] The cotton trade was enormous. In the early 1850s, 1,000 vessels a year were towed the 100 miles up the Mississippi River to New Orleans for cotton and other goods, and the trade continued after the depression of 1857–58 until interrupted by the Civil War blockade in April 1861.[29]

> Of the general carrying trades none was more important as a staple employment for American ships during this period of expansion than the cotton trade. In the shipbuilding towns, especially those in Maine, the great, bluff-bowed, flat-floored, kettle bottomed cotton freighters, the size of which rapidly increased from about 400 gross tons in 1830 to about 1,400 gross tons by 1850 … were to be seen under construction in large numbers…. The exact amount of tonnage employed cannot be determined, but it was estimated in 1852 that some 800,000 tons of American shipping employing 40,000 men were engaged in the foreign portion of this trade. This comprised about 47 per cent of the registered fleet. The new cargo carriers … had broad flat bottoms on account of the shallow water on the Mississippi bar. They also had a greater length than had been customary, and swollen sides. They proved to be good sailers, and could carry some 2,000 pounds of cotton per registered ton.[30]

The *Mary* was not built for the cotton trade, and could not carry as much cotton for her tonnage as those ships that were. She was over 1,100 tons, but could not carry 5,000 bales of cotton (2 million pounds at 400 pounds per bale). Rather, she loaded 3,400 bales (1,360,000 pounds) of cotton on her 1859 voyage, and about the same in subsequent years.[31] The amount of cotton that a ship could carry depended on its volume more than its weight, since it was so light. The bales had to be compressed to fit into the ships, which was a substantial item of expense ($2,000, or more than 50 cents per bale; later as much as 75 cents a bale). But it was a profitable trade for the *Mary* (and sometimes for the *Elizabeth Kimball* and the *Belle of the Sea*) as long as it lasted.[32]

A journal kept by Captain Bridgeo's son John (then 16 years old) begins during a passage to New Orleans from New York in 1860.[33] All goes well until on

September 7, 1860, the *Mary* strikes on Bahama Bank in a light breeze. The men carry out the best bow anchor and 90 fathoms of 11½" rope to try to pull her off, but cannot start her. They throw over cargo to lighten the ship. Wreckers from the islands come alongside and want $40,000 to put her afloat. Captain Bridgeo refuses to employ them. The next day, the 8th, continues calm and they put out 46 fathoms of chain and 46 fathoms of hawser. The wreckers are still alongside and will not help without Bridgeo giving up the ship, "which I shall not do as long as I can stand on deck and my men hold out." An underwriter's agent and another captain come on board and agree that everything possible is being done.

On September 9, they heave over more cargo. The wreckers offer the men $100 apiece to refuse to work, and tell the men that there never was a ship got off by the crew from that shoal. The captain tells the men he will pay them. The wreckers offer the captain from $5,000 to $10,000 to give the ship up at $40,000. The next day, the 10th, there is a little more wind and the men get out more line. The underwriter's agents lie a short distance away and are not allowed to render assistance by English wrecking laws.[34] On September 11, another captain comes aboard, and they heave the bow of the ship around.

Finally, on September 12, after 6 days aground, the ship begins to move and they set sail. Captain Bridgeo writes, "all afloat once more thank god from [Aloselle?] shoals." They cut hawsers, Bridgeo pays the wreckers $3,500 to get the anchors back, and they proceed to New Orleans with a light ship.[35] Captain Bridgeo and crew received

> a handsome reward from the owners and underwriters for his successful work…. A true type of old Marblehead stock, Capt. Bridgeo possessed to a marked degree all those rugged qualities which have made the race famous. He died in Marblehead in 1895, aged 76.[36]

Wrecking was a big business on both sides of the Florida Straits as ships dodged the reefs in an effort to avoid the (northward-flowing) Gulf Stream on their (southward) passage to the Gulf of Mexico. There were 47 licensed wrecking vessels on the Florida side, and 302 on the Bahamas side. Despite Captain Bridgeo's experience with attempted bribery, most wreckers were fairly honest and performed a valuable service in these treacherous waters.[37]

The *Elizabeth Kimball* also continued to make voyages, although "the mishaps attending the career of the Kimball were many."[38] The *Boston Daily Advertiser* on January 7, 1857, reported under "Disasters &c":

Ship *Elizabeth Kimball* of Beverly from Calcutta for Boston before reported to have put back into Calcutta and sld again Nov 5 [1856], had started Oct 27 and anchored at Culpee [Kulpi]. In getting under weigh next morning, the ship took a sheer [apparently, a gust of wind or current caught her as she was raising her anchor], injuring her windlass, cutwater &c. and Captain Condon took his ship back to Diamond harbor moorings [8 miles further upstream from Kulpi]. He then went to Calcutta and sent down carpenters. He left Cal. Nov 5 and it is supposed got to sea on the 9th.

In a sign of desperation, the *Elizabeth Kimball* succumbed to loading bird guano at the Chincha Islands off Peru on the way back from Melbourne in April 1861, for shipment to London as fertilizer. The guano trade was both filthy and degrading to those who participated in it, both the Chinese coolie slaves who loaded the guano, and the ships and their crews who were enveloped in the guano dust.[39] After setting out again, "in May, 1861, while bound to Cork from Callao (the port of Lima), she put into Valparaiso in distress, leaking badly," suggesting deferred maintenance as a result of poor earnings.[40]

ENDNOTES

1   Stampp (1990) pp. 223–26; Arthur H. Clark pp. 104 and 290; Hutchins p. 317; Albion (1938), p. 37.

2   Cutler (1930) p. 331.

3   Cutler (1961) p. 339.

4   Cutler (1930) p. 342.

5   Albion (1938), p. 15.

6   A vessel charter, or "contract of affreightment by charter-party," is an agreement by which a vessel or principal part of a vessel is rented to a merchant for the conveyance of goods on a voyage of pre-determined route (Flanders pp. 131ff). The owner is responsible for keeping the vessel tight, staunch and strong, and generally is responsible for supplying the master and crew, who are answerable to the owner rather than the charterer.

7   High freight rates were available for voyages to Australia, where gold had been discovered in 1851, even by non-clippers ("dull sailers") like the *Anna Kimball*.

8   Judge Sprague was born in Duxbury, Massachusetts, and was a representative and a senator from Maine in the U.S. Congress before serving as judge of the U.S. District Court for Massachusetts from 1841 to 1865. "Owing to his inability to use his eyes in reading or writing, his opinions were delivered orally" (Sprague vol. 1, 1861, Preface). He decided both the suit against Rennell and Kimball's libel against the cargo. Historian Samuel Eliot Morison commented with respect to Judge Sprague: "Laws forbidding such practices as flogging, and humane judges such as Peleg Sprague, of the District Court at Boston, could do little to alter the tradition of centuries" (Morison 1921, pp. 352–53). For another point of view, see the description by Arthur Clark, a former captain, of sea lawyers on land preying on crews and courts (Arthur H. Clark pp. 127–29).

9   *Shorey* v. *Rennell*, 22 F. Cas. 1 (D.C.D. MA 1858), Sprague, J.; same, 22 F. Cas. 6. Kimball's answer as garnishee in records of the case on microfilm at the National Archives in Waltham, MA, pp. 657–704 (1862). Kimball's full answer is lost.

10   *Rennell* v. *Kimball*, 87 MA 356 (Sup. Ct. MA 1862).

11   The Lymans had given Kimball notes dated August 31, 1857 (when the ship was in Calcutta), payable six months later. The financial panic began in October, 1857, and the Lymans failed on October 12, before the ship arrived in Boston in January 1858, without having paid the balance of the charter fee. The main issue in the case was whether the notes were given as payment (so that they replaced the maritime lien on the cargo which, unlike the notes, had value), or whether they were given as an accom-

modation, in which case the lien would continue. In connection with this issue, there was argument about the reason for the six month term of the notes, and testimony was introduced that the normal sailing time from Calcutta to Boston, and the normal time to discharge cargo in Boston, amounted to about six months, so that the notes would be surrendered for cancellation at the same time as the charter fee was payable. As noted above, Charles Marsh, who became master and part owner in 1858 (at age 47), testified that the Anna Kimball was a "dull sailer." William S. Rhoades of Marblehead, a former shipmaster, and the shipkeeper of the Anna Kimball in port, testified that he had helped paint her when she was built, agreed that she was a "very dull" sailer, and stated "I should give her five months when I should not give the Belle of the Sea over four months" to reach Boston in winter (leaving Calcutta against the southwest monsoon). He estimated a month to discharge cargo because a Calcutta cargo requires dry weather for discharging.

12 *The Anna Kimball*, 1 F. Cas. 937 (D.C. MA, 1861), rev. *Kimball* v. *The Anna Kimball*, 14 F. Cas. 481 (Cir. Ct. MA, 1861), affd. *The Kimball*, 70 U.S. 37 (1865). Microfilm records of the case at the Boston University School of Law library (roll 59 for 1865, styled *Duncan* v. *Edmund Kimball*). Presumably, one of the parties posted a bond for the cargo's value so the cargo could be sold without waiting for the final appeal.

13 He had taken that voyage to recover his eyesight after a case of measles, and it proved to be successful medicine. The book was written when he was in law school at Harvard, studying law with Justice Joseph Story.

14 Adams, p. 134. He wrote in his diary, in what sounds like self-justification: "I never have trouble with the upper class of merchants, but only with the small grinding machines and petty traders who save by small medicine chests and poor provisions" (Adams, pp. 46–47). In 1859, his health broke down and he left the practice of law for a trip around the world, which may explain why he did not argue the appeals of the *Anna Kimball* case. He later was U.S. Attorney for Massachusetts and argued one of the *Prize Cases* before Judge Peleg Sprague in the Federal District Court in Boston, and in the U.S. Supreme Court, in 1862. In these cases, the Supreme Court upheld President Lincoln's authority to blockade the Confederate states and to take Confederate vessels as prizes (Adams, pp. 266–71).

15 *Knowlton* v. *Boss* (1848), Sprague vol. 1, p.163, 14 F. Cas. 794.

16 The only exceptions to the rule were in cases where freight was lost through the fault of the owner or master, and in some circumstances where a court required payment to the crew, even though freight was not earned, as a form of salvage if a portion of the ship was saved by exertion of the crew. In some countries other than the United States, this rule was altered to provide for wages where no freight was earned if an officer of the ship certified that the crew did their duty (*The Niphon's Crew*, 18 F. Cas. 269, Cir. Ct. MA, 1849). The salvage theory was criticized in a leading maritime law text of the time: "It is difficult to perceive upon what principles of justice or humanity the

doctrine, that seamen shall be deprived of all remuneration for their services by the loss of the freight, or be compelled to rely upon the fragments of the wreck for their hard earned wages, can be maintained" (Flanders p. 341–45).

17   *The Massasoit*, 16 F. Cas. 1070 (1844).

18   Howe and Matthews under *Belle of the Sea*. Cutler (1930) p. 503 says 128 days.

19   Arthur H. Clark p. 284.

20   See also Cutler (1930) p. 342.

21   *Melbourne Age*, December 18 and 20, 1858; *Melbourne Argus*, December 18 and 20, 1858. The Arthur Clark papers at the Phillips Library contain a copy of an anonymous letter to a newspaper and an attached list of record voyages, including this one. The letter, in the *Boston Evening Traveler* for July 14, 1877, does not include the list of record voyages, and it is not clear where the list came from.

22   Morison (1921) p. 233, n. 1.

23   Cutler (1930) p. 332.

24   An account book of John Bridgeo in the Phillips Library contains some entries for the voyage of the *Mary* to San Francisco and Calcutta in 1855–57. The *Mary* had 2 junior officers and 17 men, plus a cook, a carpenter, and a steward.

25   This voyage was a profitable one. John Bridgeo's account book shows freight received in San Francisco of $16,257.15. It was before the panic of October 1857, and he remitted $10,000 to Edmund. The freights to Calcutta were $3,430.74, and to London were $19,959.96. In Cadiz, Spain, the *Mary* picked up salt for home.

26   The arrival date of September 11 given in the *Boston Shipping List* makes 112 days.

27   The *Mary*'s passage is not even listed in Cutler (1930), showing the relative obscurity of the Marblehead-built ships. The only ones included are the *Belle of the Sea*'s passages of 128 days in 1857 and 134 days in 1860.

28   Le Havre, at the mouth of the Seine, handled most of France's American trade. Like Liverpool and London, also located on tidal rivers, the docks were closed like canal locks after high tide.

29   Daggett pp. 126 and 143. In 1860, the peak year, "the tonnage under the American flag at New Orleans [outnumbered] that of foreign vessels about four to one" (Hutchins p. 321).

30   Hutchins pp. 264–65.

31   She loaded 3,269 bales in Mobile later that year (Captain Bridgeo's account book at the Phillips library). The accounts were addressed to Joseph P. Turner, who was 1/3 owner. Bridgeo was not a part owner. In contrast, Captain Jotham Blaisdell of

Kennebunk, Maine, who engaged in this trade during the years 1847–52 in a ship built for the cotton trade one half the tonnage of the *Mary* (547 v. 1,148 tons) found that he could carry 2,000 pounds of cotton per registered ton, or about a million pounds of cotton (Daggett pp. 58–63).The *Mary* was rated A1½- by American Lloyds in 1859.

32 Other large expenses of the *Mary* in 1859 were towage in and out ($1,200), stevedoring ($1,700), and port charges ($1,700). Total disbursements were over $7,000. The freight paid the *Mary* in Le Havre in April 1859 was 39,673 francs, or about $8,000 (at an exchange rate of 5 francs to the US$; see Daggett p. 125). This was an unprofitable voyage, although it was supplemented by freights from Le Havre to Boston or New York and back to New Orleans. However, in later voyages, the freight from New Orleans to Le Havre was twice as much, making the business quite profitable. Freight from Mobile to Liverpool in January 1860 was £4,325, or about $20,000 at $4.77/£. Freight from New Orleans to Le Havre in June 1860 was 111,460 francs, or about $21,000 at 5.25 francs/$ (rates are consistent with those in L. Tracy Girdler, p. 55). The *Mary* also carried 206 passengers to New York from Le Havre in July 1860.

33 Phillips Library, Microfilm 91, rolls 55–56, 1860M (1860–62, kept by John Bridgeo Jr., born 1844), 1862M (1862–63, kept by Philip Bridgeo, John Jr.'s brother, born 1846), and 1862M2 (1862–64, kept by Captain Bridgeo). An original manuscript copy of the last waterstained log (1863–64) is also in the library on microfilm. Another son, William, was born in 1849. The position given in John Bridgeo Jr.'s journal for the grounding, Lat. 26.10N Long. 75.28W, is east of Great Abaco Island in the Bahamas, near the Northeast Providence Channel and the Hole in the Wall, a common passage for ships bound for the Gulf of Mexico.

34 This may be because they were not licensed as wreckers.

35 The *Mary* was remetaled in October in New Orleans, and Bridgeo's account book shows "partial loss $17,858.56," which presumably was covered by insurance.

36 Lindsey pp. 17–18.

37 These dangers caused insurance rates for a voyage from New York to New Orleans to be more expensive than for the return trip, which simply followed the direction of the Gulf Stream (New York pp. 107, 271). Pirates had been generally put out of business in the Bahamas and the Caribbean only in the 1820s by Commodore David Porter of the U.S. Navy (Morison, 1967, pp. 97ff.). The U.S. had occupied Key West and established laws and a court to administer salvage (wrecking) operations on the Florida Keys side of the Florida Straits. More than 248 vessels were wrecked between 1849 and 1859, and there were 47 licensed wrecking vessels in 1858 (Viele, 2001, pp. 31, 34 and 54–55). On the Bahamas side of the straits, the figures were even larger. Some 300 vessels were wrecked between 1845 and 1870, and there were 302 licensed wrecking vessels in 1856 (Albury pp. 135, 137 and 141). Under maritime law, if a captain agreed to give his ship over to the wreckers, the salvage payment to the wreckers was usually

40 to 60 percent of the value of the vessel and cargo, depending on a number of factors, but if the wreckers were unsuccessful, they received nothing.

38   Howe and Matthews, under *Elizabeth Kimball.*

39   "The guano trade was debasing and degrading to the captains and to their clippers. To the coolies who dug the stuff, it was death. The coolies had come from China to labor for the Peruvian government for a period of five years.... [T]hey were housed in rude cane huts, grossly underfed, and given only rags to wear. They were worked by brutal overseers from sunrise to sunset, seven days a week. Those who did not die from starvation, exhaustion, or breathing guano dust, committed suicide by jumping from the cliffs into the sea.... For captains forced to wait months to take on their cargoes, there was nothing but boredom and helpless fury.... When at last it came a clipper's turn to be loaded, she was drawn up close to a cliff. Coolies, their mouths and noses covered with thick bandages, shoveled the guano into sleevelike chutes that led directly into the ship's hold. All the while, the vessel was enveloped in a cloud of yellow, reeking guano dust that penetrated everywhere, tarnishing brass and silver and covering all with its pollution.... It usually took a week at sea to get a ship clean, and the upper spars and tackle stayed yellow until she got into the rainy weather off Patagonia. The memory of the murderous slavery on the Chinchas could never be so easily washed away" (Lyon, 1962, pp. 121–23). See also Rowe pp. 222–23.

40   The ship was rated A1 in 1859 by American Lloyds, but A2 in 1861.

TEN

FINAL DISASTERS &c., 1861–67

THE CIVIL WAR, WHICH BEGAN IN APRIL 1861, on the heels of the 1857 depression, had a further disastrous effect on American shipping. The cotton trade out of New Orleans and other ports was eliminated by the blockade of southern ports ordered by President Lincoln. At least five hundred ships therefore had to find other employment.[1] Captain Whidden was in Rio de Janeiro when war was declared, and recalled that "it was not only the Southerners who were troubled in mind; the flag was shut down on, and freights were not obtainable for Yankee bottoms without great difficulty."[2] War risk insurance was needed to protect against the depredations of Confederate raiders.[3] The Marblehead ships did what they could to keep profitably employed, but at some point in 1862 or 1863, Edmund Kimball made a decision to wind up his shipping business. He sold his one third interest in the Mary to Joseph P. Turner (who owned another third), and tried to sell the *Belle of the Sea*, but without success.[4]

The turning point was probably receipt of a letter from Captain Grindle of the *Elizabeth Kimball*.

Hong Kong, Feb. 28th, 1863
Edmund Kimball Esq.
      Boston.
      Dear Sir:

I left Shanghae the 17th inst. mouth of the river, and arrived here the 21st inst. By the enclosed charter party, you will see my present employment. It is the best charter that has been given here this season. I have made my freight payable in gold, which will be greatly in our favor if the prem. keeps up. If possible, I shall pay all my disbursements in San Francisco in legal tender paper and save the prem. on my gold. I shall have to caulk here from copper up, and the decks. I shall endeavor to always make my expenses light as possible.

Shanghae is a very expensive port, and everything is monstrous high. Beef is fifteen cents pr. pound, potatoes, four dollars a picul, and everything else in proportion. The great difference of exchange which I had to allow to make Mexican dollars (which is the only currency in Shanghae) equivalent to U.S. currency, according to charter party, brought the balance of our freight so low, that I was obliged to draw on you for $750. to clear my ship. It was an unfortunate charter. Had the charter been made payable in Mexican dollars, and no allowance taken in New York, we should have saved 33 1/3 pr cent on whole charter, which would have amounted to $4,357., about, more than enough to disburse the ship in Shanghae!

In Shanghae, I sent you copy of extended protest, and the General Average Adjustment, which will enable you to collect insurance of freight jettisoned.[5] Should it not come to hand, Messrs Fogg Bros. Burlingship, New York, have the duplicates, sent them by their House in Shanghae, as they were interested with Jewett & Co. in our charter. I also now enclose your copy of my charter, and a correct account of ship. There is one omission; by some carelessness of my consignee, a bill of $409. for shipping new crew, cook and steward, was not charged, which I did not notice until I got to sea. If they draw on me here, I shall have to pay it. This bill was one months advance wages and shipping fees. By my sailors running away in Shanghae, the ship saved about $500.00 in wages and provisions, after deducting what I had given them. The ship will have that much left to pay in San Francisco. Sailors wages in Shanghae is $25. But I shipped them for only one month, and not until I was ready to leave; so when that month is up, I can discharge them, for sailors wages here is only $15. Had my crew staid by in Shanghae, my provision marketing would have been heavy, and their wages all the time going on! All the sailors ran away but three. Shanghae is a very sickly place, and all ships have a physician tend the ship by the month, which is much cheaper than to send a man to the hospital, or send for doctor by the visit at $5 each time. One of my men was so far gone that he could not be treated on board, and he was in the hospital forty three days at one tael pr. day. He afterwards deserted. Every ship also has to hire a sampan by the month (China boat and man) to wait upon the ship, take the Captain on shore to his business, from one place to another.

When I was ready, I could not charter in Shanghae. The "Almena" had been laying on the berth six months for New York, and not full when I left. Cotton had advanced so high in Shanghae just before I left, that they could not ship one bale here. When I first arrived there, ships were getting full cargoes for here at $1 per bale, small cotton.

If I receive no further orders from you in San Francisco, I will make your remittance to Baring Bros & Co. London. I have received no letters from you in China.

I am dear Sir,
Your Obed't. Serv't.

J.S. Grindle

The letter—a classic case of putting the good news first—shows the devastating effect of the financial uncertainty caused by the war. The premium on gold over paper methods of payment during the Civil War would culminate in a gold premium of 100 percent in 1864.[6] At the time of Grindle's letter, Mexican gold dollars were at a premium of 1/3 over paper money. When the *Elizabeth Kimball* arrived in San Francisco in June 1863, Kimball sold her to Pope and Talbot for use in hauling timber on the west coast.[7]

But it was not easy to wind up a shipping business quickly and without further loss during those hard times. Kimball still had promises to keep.

On February 24, 1863, a newspaper stated that Simon McKay and Ben Dutton had moved to Charlestown, where they were finding plenty of business and were building a ship of one thousand tons burden for Edward Kimball Esq. [sic].[8]

This was to be the *Lady Washington*, built in Boston and registered in New York by Edmund on August 25, 1863. Soon after she was launched, Edmund sold her, on February 20, 1864, in San Francisco.[9]

Voyage of the *Mary* from Calcutta to Boston via London

The *Mary*, under Captain Bridgeo, made a middling voyage from Boston to San Francisco and then on to Calcutta in 1862. While at anchor at San Francisco in a gale on September 4, 1862, Captain Bridgeo abandons his usual terseness in the log and writes: "She commenced dragging let go port anchor immediately still continued dragging and as she would on turn of tide be foul of a [Federal] gunboat lying at anchor, gave her a sheer [hauled anchors short] set the mizzen topsail and back her into a clear berth and brought to with 45 fathoms starboard anchor and thirty fathoms port one"—a slick maneuver. John Bridgeo Jr. (now 18 years old) put some detail in his journal for May 25, 1862, rounding the horn, "At 11 pm while letting a reef out of the topsls Jefferson Phillips seaman of Wells Maine fell from the fore yard striking on the fore hatch fractured his scull and died in 15 minutes he leaves a good chest of clothes and $15 in bank notes." The captain's log for the same event was characteristically terse: "A man by the name of Jefferson Phillips fell from the fore yard—dead on deck."

A series of letters from Captain Bridgeo to Joseph P. Turner give a vivid description of this final voyage of the *Mary* as a Marblehead-owned ship from Calcutta to London and on in 1863–64, as Turner attempted to sell the ship.[10]

> [Calcutta 1/3/1863] This voyage has been a hard one for expenses but I hope I shall be able to give you satisfaction which is my only aim, for if I do not make any money for you this voyage I shall feel almost discouraged myself.

> [Calcutta 1/8/63] I have sold a draft on Isac Rich [Boston banker] of 3,500 rupees at 70 cts per rupee which is awful but it's the best we could do.[11]

> [London 5/18/63] [I]f you should send her on a long voyage she will require coppering and entire new suit of sails and a considerable part of her standing rigging has parted and of course you would have to replace that, which would cost a great deal to fit her out.... You would sell her better at home.... You are rather higher in your value of the *Mary* than she would bring here ... I am positively sure you would have to spend a great amount of money on her to get her classed at Lloyds.

> [London 6/13/63] There is never a ship sold here, but there is something to detain the Capt. for a long time. They have made a practice as soon as they pay in 10 % to put a man on board and there hardly a ship that has lost something by the time the rest of the money becomes due.... For that reason I have refused that privilege.... The reason I think they may have or find something that is not necessary for them to know.

> [London 6/20/63] I do not like laying still.

[London 6/27/63] Ships seem to be a drug in the market, and great many has been taking out and chartered that was for sale. I think we could take £6,200 for the *Mary*, but your limits are so that we cannot take it … I know exactly what the ship is, as I have been in her ever since she was launched. *I have taken this liberty to write*, the ship is rotten in a greater part, although I say nothing about it here, and of course I cover it over in every way.

[London 7/11/63] About all the American ships are changing their flags to Bremen and Hamburg.

[London 8/1/63] I have discharged my two boys … one of my boys goes to India[12] and the other is coming home.

[Cardiff Roads, Wales 9/21/63; had charter to carry coal from Cardiff to Gibraltar] I have the ship loaded and in the stream ready for sea but its blowing a heavy gale of wind from the WNW and we are riding with two anchors ahead with 75 fathoms of chain on each.… I have in 1,635 tons of coal making £1,430,2.6 freight.… The ships copper is very bad and she makes about 27 inches of water in 24 hours which annoys me very much but I hope she will shrink up some but at all events I shall go to sea with her as she is. I am very glad I have no Marblehead men with [me] although I dare say I shall get through the voyage very well.… I find by laying so long in London its played the mischief my running rigging although the most part of it was below.… Sept. 23 Its blowing heavy and I have just lost my port anchor. The chain parted about two fathoms from the ring.… Sept 26 I am [north] of Sunday Island … everything was so contrary I feel almost discouraged.

[Gibraltar 10/20/63] I arrived here yesterday after a very rough passage of 18 days from Cardiff with the loss of a main topsail and have bursted almost every old sail I had on the ship, for I never saw so much sea and wind for 16 days in succession in my life. It of course caused the ship to strain a great deal. We carried away the fore and main topmast backstay but I shall knot them and try to get her home with them as it will cost a great deal of money here … as I have often said I should run her as long as she would go, I shall try to get her home but Mr. Turner she will be very expensive on you when she gets there.… The ship makes about 11 inches an hour which makes it very disagreeable to get along with sailors here especially with such men as we get now days in the European trade.

[Gibraltar 10/31/63] Crew all left the ship without permission having deserted taking all their clothes with them. [They were not Marblehead men, but they knew an unsound ship when they saw one.]

[Cadiz Roads 12/30/63; loaded with salt] I have had a great deal of trouble with my crew as they refused duty on the account of the ship leaking causing me to call a survey which has ordered me to take six men more which I have done.[13]

[St. Thomas, Virgin Islands 2/6/1864] I wrote you on the date of Jan. 30th by the way of Jamaica that I had been obliged to put into this port with the ship leaking at the rate of 30 inches of water an hour, and with the loss jibboom fore topgalt. mast and all our back stays fore and aft … at 8 am [Jan. 21] we tried the pump and found the ship to have 4 feet of water in the hold. I immediately put all hands to the pump and after pumping 6 hours, we pumping with both pumps and keeping the ship before the wind, we freed her to 17 inches, all hands being on deck 18 hours. I sent one half below and the others to the pumps, and from that time up to this date the pump has not ceased, on the 21st the men refused to pump any longer without I put her for the nearest port and my officers the same. I was forced to give way although much against my will but had I had a cargo in that would have stood the water without perishing I should not have put in…. On the first day after I got here I put a sail under her and stopped the leak some for about 24 hours, and since that time she makes about the same water as when I arrived. [Chartered vessels to take salt to Boston]… As she is at present I think its infeasible to move her, I have 16 men pumping night and day…. I feel in regard to this work that it will never end and for my employees I hardly know which way to turn for this a sad affair.

[St. Thomas 2/13/64] The ship makes about 18 to 20 inches of water per hour causing both pumps to be kept agoing two thirds of the time. I have all my men by me and a gang of pumpers night and day which makes it very expensive and I would have rejoiced if she had gone down under me rather than been in here in this situation but as I am here I hope I shall be able to perform this business to your satisfaction and also the satisfaction of the underwriters.

[St. Thomas 3/14/64] The ship continues to make 30 inches of water an hour.

[St. Thomas 3/30/64] I have the ship caulked on one side and hope to finish the other this week. She now lays with her keel out of water with her starboard side up. Her bottom is very open although nothing to compare with the garboard. I can take an iron and with my hands put it right through. I feel surprised to see how she was kept afloat, as she did. I feel in hopes that I shall be able to leave this place next week for it appears to me I can see daylight through this miserable job. You must excuse my not writing by the last opportunity as I was very unwell at the time and having the ship on her side at the time caused me a great anxiety…. I shall do nothing to her but caulk and replace the rigging that is parted.

The *Mary* was sold to a Boston firm when she reached Boston on April 30, 1864. Captain Bridgeo, who in Marblehead fashion never became more than "almost discouraged" through all of these troubles, in 1866 took command of the barque *Hellespont* and sailed to Zanzibar, Aden, and Muscat—exciting new ports for him.

At the same time that Joseph Turner was receiving all of this bad news, and probably wishing he had taken Capt. Bridgeo's advice and sold the *Mary* in London for less than originally asked, Captain Freeto decided to sell the "good ship *Riga*" for £4,100 in Aberdeen, Scotland, in early 1864.[14]

The *Belle of the Sea*'s Voyage to San Francisco and Calcutta

The sale of the *Belle of the Sea* took longer and was more complicated. She was finally sold in 1867, as a result of a series of transactions that mark the end of Marblehead's shipping business, and of Kimball's fortune. On or about March 18, 1867, the ship left Calcutta under charter for New York. She subsequently sprung a leak during a severe three-day storm and put into Mauritius for repairs. Two letters from Houdlette and Perkins there were received by Kimball. The first, dated May 6, 1867, advises that the ship was making about 9 inches of water an hour and needed to discharge her cargo for examination. They agreed to take the captain's drafts on Baring Bros. and Co., London, together with a bottomry bond as collateral security for the repairs. Bottomry is an odd combination of a mortgage and a credit insurance policy, derived from Roman law and founded on the necessities of ocean voyages:

> Bottomry is a contract by which the ship, or, as it used to be said, the keel or bottom of the ship is pledged to secure the payment of money borrowed by the owner to fit her for sea, repair her, etc.; and the agreement is, that if the ship is lost by any of the perils enumerated in the contract, the lender loses his money; but if the ship arrives safely, or is in safety at the termination of the time stipulated for the repayment of the loan, he is to receive back his principal sum and a marine interest, at the rate agreed upon, though it exceeds the legal interest.[15]

The first letter from Mauritius also says that "on account of an epidemic fever which has been raging in Mauritius for the last three months causing a great mortality, the cost of repairing the vessel, owing to a scarcity of laborers, would be greater than formerly." The second letter, dated June 6, 1867, advises that large leaks were found in the garboard strake and her caulking was found very slack. They estimate the disbursements to be [an indecipherable amount, but probably less than the event], and note that Captain Hammond has the fever. In the event, the captain had to execute a bottomry bond for $29,444.05 in Mauritius currency, plus 13½ percent marine interest or premium (effectively, the cost of the bond). This extreme amount was later converted to $46,805.31 in U.S. currency at a time when gold was at a 43 percent premium to the U.S. dollar. The repairs cost three times more than any prior refit, and more than the value of the ship, because of the depreciated U.S. dollar.

Upon arrival of the ship in New York on or about October 13, 1867, a lien on the bottomry bond attached to the *Belle of the Sea* and her cargo. In a complicated series of transactions, the claims of the various parties with an interest in the ship, the cargo and the freight were adjusted resulting in a balance of $5,271.99 owed by the ship, which had been sold at auction.[16]

The *Anna Kimball*'s Voyage to Shanghai and Nagasaki

The *Anna Kimball* eked out a living during the Civil War as a twelve-year-old transient freighter.[17] On her last voyage, on April 12, 1867, the *Anna Kimball*, Captain Williams, left Shanghai for Nagasaki, Japan, chartered "under sealed orders" by prince Kurumo of Japan.[18] She arrived at Nagasaki during the turbulent period leading up to the deposition of the Shogun (the hereditary military dictator who ruled in the name of the emperor) and the restoration of the emperor Meiji in 1868. In 1853–54, Commodore Perry of the U.S. Navy had negotiated the opening of two Japanese ports for the first time after some 240 years of complete isolation from the West. Now, there was trouble between various princes and the "Tycoon" (as Westerners at that time called the Shogun).[19] The American consul wanted to bring the *Anna Kimball* into port, but given the political uncertainty the captain refused unless he received orders to do so from the charterer. The "Tycoon" delivered a summons to surrender the ship, but captain Williams said he would shoot anyone coming on board, as he was in navigable waters. Mr. Lake, apparently the agent of the charterer on board, ordered the ship to sail to Shanghai and there await further orders. She left Shanghai for Nagasaki again on May 15, and on May 31, the U.S. Marshall on the U.S. Steamer *Wyoming* ordered the captain to give up the ship for "unlawfully obtaining cargo." She was towed into Nagasaki and was

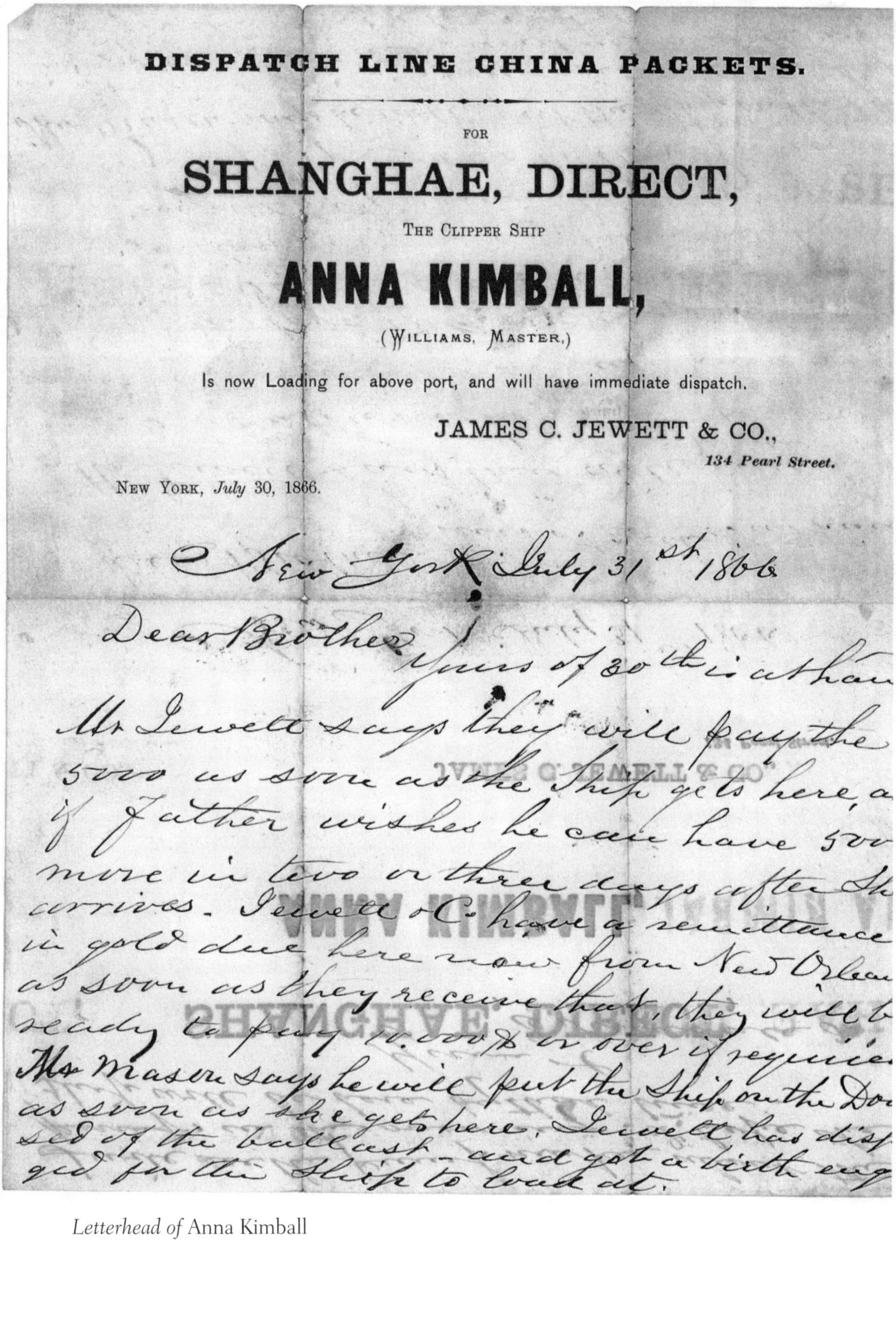

DISPATCH LINE CHINA PACKETS.

FOR

SHANGHAE, DIRECT,

THE CLIPPER SHIP

ANNA KIMBALL,

(WILLIAMS, MASTER,)

Is now Loading for above port, and will have immediate dispatch.

JAMES C. JEWETT & CO.,

134 Pearl Street.

NEW YORK, *July 30, 1866.*

New York July 31st 1866

Dear Brother Yours of 30th is at hand
Mr Jewett says they will pay the
500 as soon as the Ship gets here, a[nd]
if Father wishes he can have 500
more in two or three days after Sh[e]
arrives. Jewett & Co have a remittance
in gold due here now from New Orlea[ns]
as soon as they receive that, they will b[e]
ready to pay 1000$ or over if require[d]
Mr Mason says he will put the Ship on the Do[ck]
as soon as she gets here, Jewett has dis[po]
sed of the ballast and got a birth eng[a]
ged for the Ship to load at.

Letterhead of Anna Kimball

Marblehead Harbor. North side. Courtesy of Peabody Essex Museum.

charged with "smuggling in a nonopened port" and fined $1,000 (it appears that the *Anna Kimball* was attempting to import rice, whose cost in Japan had increased manyfold).[20] The fine was paid by the attorney for the charterer and the charge was withdrawn. Captain Williams noted tersely in his log: "Thus ends the great rice voyage in Japan and all difficulty."

In November 1868 the *Anna Kimball* left Shanghai for Batavia, Java, and on December 1, she ran aground off Gaspar Island, a treacherous area for ships.[21] As Joseph Conrad says in *Typhoon*: "The China seas north and south are narrow seas. They are seas full of every-day eloquent facts, such as islands, sand-banks, reefs, swift and changeable currents—tangled facts that nevertheless speak to a seaman in clear and definite language."[22] The *Anna Kimball* got off, making 10″ of water an hour, but upon inspection in Batavia it is found that "the forefoot is badly injured, also a portion of shoe gone, copper badly damaged to the waist of the ship. After part seems to be not in a bad condition as far as could be ascertained through divers." The ship was surveyed and sold in Liverpool in September 1868, completing the sale of the Marblehead ships.

Many shipowners, like Kimball, had "lost nearly all [their] money" when the clipper ship bubble burst.[23] The next generation of Marbleheaders, like that of other coastal towns, turned their attention to manufacturing and westward expansion.

> Given equal energy and intelligence, the man who once commanded
> a ship or conducted a small overseas trading concern could with less risk
> and hardship control the destinies of a sizeable inland empire.[24]

ENDNOTES

1   Assuming the thousand-odd trips up the Mississippi to New Orleans each year were by ships making two voyages a year. Other cotton ports were also blockaded.

2   Whidden p. 201; Hutchins p. 323. Later, Whidden concluded: "…[A]s a war measure our tariff was increased on everything pertaining to shipping as well as everything else, which was a deathblow for the time to American ships, the tariff being prohibitory to competition with foreign shipping. Not having a force to protect our merchant marine, the greater part were placed under a foreign flag, mostly English, for protection. Those that remained and still swung 'Old Glory' from their peaks, became a prey to Southern privateers—the 'Alabama,' 'Shenandoah,' and others, while those that escaped capture were relegated to distant ports to pick up a precarious livelihood until the war was over" (pp. 310–11).

3   In 1883, Edmund's son Charles filed a claim in the Court of Commissioners of *Alabama* Claims for the cost of war risk insurance purchased by Edmund during the Civil War. Twenty Confederate cruisers, such as the *Florida* and the *Alabama*, destroyed 257 Union ships. The *Alabama* was finally destroyed by the Union vessel *Kearsage* in a battle off France in 1864. In 1872 the Geneva Tribunal of Arbitration decided that Great Britain had breached its treaty obligations of neutrality in aiding Confederate ships (the *Alabama* had been built in Birkenhead, near Liverpool) and awarded the United States $15.5 million for damages. These damages were distributed to claimants by the Court of Commissioners of *Alabama* Claims. The first court did not distribute all the money available to people whose ships had been destroyed, so a second court was established by Congress to distribute the remaining money to people who had had to buy war risk insurance because of the Confederate cruisers. In 1885, after Edmund's death, his son Charles (then 40) was awarded $3,307.17 with $1,817.11 in interest. Letter dated February 10, 2000, from National Archives at College Park, referring to NWCTC (room 2600), RG59, 250/54/10/07, Docket Book R, page 4855.

4   American Lloyds, 1862. In 1865 American Lloyds shows the *Mary* as being owned by Bates and Co., Boston.

5   [Footnote supplied by author:] General Average derived from the maritime law of Rhodes dating from 900 B.C. If cargo is jettisoned to save a ship, and the ship is saved thereby, upon reaching port the ship and the rest of the cargo must all share the value of the cargo that is lost. *Barnard v. Adams*, 51 U.S. 270 (U.S. Sup. Ct. 1850). General Average computations could be complex, and were often carried out by expert average adjusters.

6   An article in the *Economist* of London on November 8, 1856 (reprinted in *The Living Age* 658, January 3, 1857, p. 54) entitled "The Exchanges with the East," just prior to

the panic of 1857, had noted that, as a result of the large trade deficit between Britain and the Far East, "the rate at which bills [or exchange] on England from their abundance are saleable is so disadvantageous, that it becomes profitable to transmit silver from [Britain], either as a direct means of payment for the exports from China, or as an exchange operation, to purchase the bills drawn upon London and offered for sale in China." A January 1865 article in the *North American Review* (entitled "The National Resources, and their Relation to Foreign Commerce and the Price of Gold," 100: 206, p. 126), noted the growth of the premium on gold from zero prior to July 1862 to 109 percent in June 1864. The article argued that the premium did not signify "commercial exhaustion and dependence," but was "an anomaly, a circumstance altogether different from the apparently similar circumstances in the history of other nations," or "is the result of alarms and speculations, rather than of commercial transactions." It seems likely that the sudden increase in the gold premium (set by the market for exchange) in 1837, 1857 and 1863–64, in each case was attributable primarily to financial stress and uncertainty.

7   Kimball's son Charles was asked in 1883: "Do you know what was the value of your father's property during the war?" His answer, under oath, was: "Only that he told me that he was worth $40,000—that was in 1862, I think. He had $40,000 in government bonds, and he could sell his vessels for transports so as to have $40,000" (*Alabama* claim deposition). The end of the *Elizabeth Kimball* came in 1873, when she was beached on the isolated Easter Island, in the South Pacific, with 15 feet of water in the hold. The crew built a ten-ton schooner from the wreck, and the Captain, his wife, and eight others who wished to leave reached Tahiti, 2,550 miles away, in 24 days (Howe and Matthews).

8   Cheney, pp. 129 and 181. Ben Dutton apparently had returned to Newburyport after building the *Belle of the Sea* and a few schooners in 1858, and in 1861 "sailed for the James River to cut ship timber for himself and Simon McKay."

9   Soon after that, the *Lady Washington* was "Struck by a squall, dragged anchor and was wrecked on a reef May 3, 1864, while loading guano at Baker's Island, Pacific Ocean" (card at the Bostonian Society Library, Old State House, Boston).

10   In the Turner file at the Marblehead Museum and Historical Society. Brackets and footnotes are the current author's.

11   The earlier exchange rate was 53 cents per rupee.

12   The younger son, Philip, continued on the ships *Revely* and *Golden Fleece*.

13   Seamen could insist upon a survey of a vessel on the ground of unseaworthiness, and the cost could not be imposed on them if there was reasonable cause for the survey (Flanders p. 416).

14   Letter dated December 15, 1863, from Captain Freeto to Turner in Turner file,

Marblehead Museum and Historical Society.

15   *Knott P. Bray v. Bates*, 50 MA 237, 250, Sup. Ct. Mass. 1845. Bottomry was intended
     to give the master of a ship in foreign ports a means of obtaining funds to repair the
     ship or obtain supplies and continue the voyage. The master had implied authority to
     borrow on bottomry if the expenditure was necessary, and if it was necessary to borrow
     on bottomry to cover the expenditure because the owner did not have normal credit
     in the strange port (*The Aurora*, 14 U.S. 96, U.S. Sup. Ct. 1816, Story, J). The lender
     could charge "marine interest," which really was an insurance premium rather than
     normal interest, and was not subject to usury laws prohibiting large rates of interest,
     because the lender could only recover on the bottomry bond if the vessel reached home
     port safely. The lender was also at risk if the value of the ship was insufficient to cover
     the bottomry bond (*The Ship Virgin* v. *Vyfhius*, 33 U.S. 538, U.S. Sup. Ct. 1834, Story,
     J.)

16   Because Nickerson (the new owner) did not pay this, Johnson and Higgins filed suit,
     and three levels of courts, including the U.S. Supreme Court, held after seven years of
     litigation that Johnson and Higgins could recover (*Johnson* v. *Belle of the Sea*, 13 F.Cas.
     730, Cir. Ct. E.D.Pa. 1872, aff'd. *Belle of the Sea*, 87 U.S. 421, 428, U.S. Sup. Ct.
     1874). Whatever may have been said between the parties, it is clear that Edmund and
     Nickerson felt cheated by Johnson and Higgins.

17   Twenty years was the normal limit of the active life of a sailing vessel (Albion p. 98),
     but the average age was only 8–10 years (Dean, 2001, p. 39). A log book now in the
     Phillips Library covers the period beginning April 1, 1864, when the ship is in Dundee
     on the southeast coast of Scotland, on a voyage to Boston and then Montevideo,
     Uruguay, ending on December 16, 1864.

18   Blunt White Library at the Mystic Seaport Museum, Log No. 685. Kurume is near
     Nagasaki, about 500 miles from Shanghai.

19   In the name of the emperor, the "hereditary Tycoon or Shogun of the house of
     Tokugawa had governed since 1600" (Morison, 1967, p. 277).

20   Beasley (1963) pp. 76–78.

21   The straits of Gaspar, now called the Gelasa Straits, lie between Bangka and Belitung,
     formerly Gaspar Island and St. John's Island, east of Sumatra. In October 1856 it took
     the clipper ship *Charmer* four days tacking into the southerly monsoon to get through
     "the abominable *Straits of Gaspar* the *bugbear* of these parts." In April 1860, the clipper
     ship *Intrepid* ran on Belvidere shoal at the entrance to the Gaspar straits and was lost.
     (Gosnell, 1989, pp. 93 and 253–57). The available charts contained errors, and many
     other ships suffered the same fate (MacGregor pp. 20ff). If ships avoided the reefs,
     they still had to worry about the spears of the Malay pirates, as they had worried about
     pirates at an earlier time in traversing the Florida Straits (Whidden pp. 39, 216–18;
     Connolly, 1943, p. 117). Of all the voyages of Edmund's ships to the Far East, par-

ticularly Calcutta, none were made to Canton or other Chinese ports except these last voyages of the *Anna Kimball* and *Elizabeth Kimball* to Singapore, Shanghai and Hong Kong, during and after the Civil War.

22   (1902), chapter 1.

23   In a March 10, 1883, letter to his brother Charles, John R. Kimball wrote: "It seems strange and dreamlike that we whose lives began so brightly and were scarcely clouded when these [war risk] insurances were effected should now, in our mid years, and facing the decline of life, be compelled to look with so much hope to even such a pittance as this War Claim at the largest must be."

24   Cutler (1930) p. 310.

Appendix A:

Letter to Major General Lincoln from Colonel Azor Orne, October 18, 1782[1]

Marblehead Oct. 18th, 1782

Dear Sir

Agreeably to your request as stated in your letter of the 27th of Sept. I have endeavoured to answer the questions therein stated as they respect the codfishery at Marblehead before the War.

The number of vessels were about one hundred fifty.

Their size from thirty to seventy tons three quarters of them the largest size.

The worth on an average was four hundred fifty pounds.

The number of men employed from seven to eight including boys.

The sum annually required to keep each vessel in repair pay insurance and raise a sufficient sum to replace the vessel when rendered unfit for service one hundred pounds.

The quantity of fish caught on an average one thousand quintals.

The proportion of the year those vessels were employed eight months.

The articles called great general were salt, bait, candle soap and tallow charges against the whole stock of fish taken.

The articles of small general were wood, cyder, flour and other small stores and were charged against the men and lads employed in the vessels.

The average price of fish 15/6 [15 shillings and sixpence].

It required ten men to cure ten vessels fish.

The worth of the land on which flakes were built for ten vessels sixty pounds being in general unfit for any other use.

The worth of the buildings and flakes for ten vessels was six hundred pounds.

The annual expense of repairs sixty pounds for ten.

The vessels in the winter were some of them employed in bringing grain etc. from the southern colonies some to the West Indies and others to Spain and Portugal.

Very few hired out.

I am my dear Gen. Your Obedient and Obliged Humble Servant,
    Major General Lincoln   S. Orne

P.S. Now sir should this branch of business be taken from us in the settlement of a peace our commerce is at an end in this State as we have no other export of any consequence and where there are no exports it is impossible there should be great imports I will not at this time undertake to state the disadvantages that would arise to this State in particular the new England States or the United States in gen. But the task not difficult should a deprivation of the fishery be our fate rather than submit to it I should be for continuing the war until there was no men left. Then we should have no occasion for commerce[,] but you say I am warm[,] and should you[,] I shall answer that the fortitude and patriotism of such men as Gen. Lincoln has perhaps had some tendency to assist my natural inclination to be independent.

1 From Turner file, Marblehead Museum and Historical Society

Appendix B:

Number of Vessels Employed in the Confishery at Marblehead, 1794–1850[1]

Year	Above 50 tons	Under 50 tons	Year	Above 50 tons	Under 50 tons
1794	48	21	1826	45	30
1795	48	24	1827	54	31
1796	47	25	1828	57	28
1797	50	28	1829	57	46
1798	49	32	1830	51	15
1799	46	27	1831	52	17
1800	37	32	1832	49	19
1801	59	24	1833	59	21
1802	65	26	1834	58	13
1803	86	12	1835	66	8
1804	84	16	1836	58	3
1805	83	16	1837	62	3
1806	84	17	1838	69	6
1807	98	18	1839	95	3
1808	77	17	1840	83	4
1809	54	13	1841	70	4
1810	39	13	1842	64	4
1811	51	15	1843	66	5
1812	41	23	1844	67	7
1813	0	23	1845	64	4
1814	0	31	1846	46	6
1815	30	18	1847	23	4
1816	52	12	1848	29	13
1817	69	9	1849	24	10
1818	83	17	1850	23	7
1819	90	21			
1820	59	22			
1821	40	26			
1822	51	25			
1823	52	31			
1824	48	29			
1825	56	33			

[1] Handwritten list in Turner file, Marblehead Museum and Historical Society.

Appendix C:

Chronological List of Vessels Owned by Edmund Kimball of Marblehead[1]

AL	American Lloyd's Register of American and Foreign Shipping
B	built (place and year)
bark or barque	a three-masted square-rigged vessel with a fore-and-aft mizzen
BH	billethead (scrollwork on the bow)
brig	a two-masted square-rigged vessel
C	captain
D	depth
EK	Edmund Kimball
H	history
M'head FT	registered in Marblehead for foreign rather than coastal trade
O	owner/s
R	registered
schooner	a two masted fore-and-aft gaff-rigged vessel with main aft
ship	a three-masted square-rigged vessel
W	width

America   schooner   71 feet   104 tons   D 7' 8"
> B New Castle, NH 1801
> R 1817, 1822, 1829 M'head foreign trade
> C William Frost, William Tufts (1822), John Stover (1829)
> O Edmund Kimball (EK) and Arnold Martin III, EK only (1822)
> H 1842 owned by Crowell, Collins, Baker, Crowell. Robert Atkins died at sea
> 1822, Benj Graves, Master

Mechanic   schooner   55 feet   53 tons   D 6' 9"
> B Newbury 1823
> R 1823, 1833, 1836 M'head FT, also 1823 Newburyport
> C John High, Thomas P. Hammond (1833), William Roads (1836), Philip
> Meservey (1836)

Hope   schooner   61 feet   85 tons   D 9' 1"
   B Newbury 1825
   R 1825 M'head
   H 1831 owned by John P. Creesey

Garland   schooner   55 feet   60 tons   D 7' 9"
   B Essex 1822
   R 1826 M'head
   C Samuel Snow
   H 1828 owned by William Reed etc.

Eliza   schooner   55 feet   55 tons   D 7' 5"
   B Essex 1819
   R 1826, 1831, 1833 M'head FT
   C William D. Hammond, Philip Brigeo (1831), John Lecraw (1833), John
      Leenam (1833)
   O EK and John Dexter, EK only (1831)

Plough Boy   schooner   49 feet   73 tons   D 7' 8"
   B Amesbury 1803
   R 1826 M'head
   C Joseph A. Hooper, Philip Bessom (1829)

Plough Boy   schooner   63 feet   98 tons   D 7' 8"
   B Amesbury 1803
   R 1828, 1829 M'head
   C William Hammond (1828), Philip Bessom (1829), Samuel Graves (1829)
   H 1828 apparently altered from 49 feet. 1831 owned by Josiah P. Creesy, father
      of captain of clipper *Flying Cloud*

Lewis   schooner   48 feet   74 tons   D 8'
   B Newbury 1804
   R 1830, 1831 M'head
   C Ephraim Cousins, Joseph I. Arnold (1831)
   H 1819 owned by William Russell, captain, son of John Roads Russell. 1827
      appears in account book (charter?)

Fair America   sloop   72 feet   99 tons   D 7' 1"
  B Waldoboro, ME 1820
  R 1827, 1830, 1835 M'head
  C John H. Cousins, Samuel Snow (1830)
  O EK and Jeremiah Fogg of Richard, ME
  H 1830 altered to schooner. 1835 owned by Appleton, Bullfinch, Fogg

Sally   schooner   62 feet   82 tons   D 8' 9"
  B Danvers 1800
  R 1828, 1829, 1839 M'head FT, also Newburyport 1828
  C Philip Bridgeo, Mark H. Messervey (1839)

Mary   schooner   74 feet   106 tons   D 7' 3"
  B Newbury 1826
  R 1829, 1830, 1832 M'head
  C John H. Cousins, William S. Loud (1832)

Splendid   schooner   57 feet   63 tons   D 7' 6"
  B Essex 1829
  R 1829 M'head
  C Samuel Snow
  H 1831 lost at sea with Snow, Ramsdell, Selman, Adams, Dennis, Millet

Quero   schooner   63 feet   66 tons   D 6' 8"
  B Newbury 1828
  R 1832 M'head
  C Philip Bridgeo
  H Probably named for Bank Quereau. 1848 owned by Billing P. Hardy and John
    Adams

Sophonia   schooner   69 feet   89 tons   D 8'
  B Amesbury 1816
  R 1832 M'head
  C Philip Bridgeo
  O EK and Philip Bridgeo

Edward   schooner   65 feet   84 tons   D 8'
    B Essex 1833
    R 1833 M'head
    C Edward Dixey
    H 1839 owned by Ed Crowninshield and Edward Dixey

William   schooner   69 feet   97 tons   D 8' 7"   BH
    B Essex 1833
    R 1833, 1834, 1835, 1836, 1837, 1842, 1843 M'head FT
    C Philip A. Meservey, Philip Bridgeo (1834–37), John G. Stacey (1842), Philip
       B. Graves (1843)
    H Probably named for EK's son William, d. 1829 age 8. 1838 Owned by George
       Wilson and John Chandler Jr; in 1842 by EK again. Alexander McIntosh
       "drowned in the Harbour from Sch William" 1836

Daniel Baxter   schooner   79 feet   133 tons   D 8' 4"
    B Prospect, ME 1830
    R 1833 M'head FT
    C Asa Hooper, Jr. (Mary Kimball's brother)

Maraposa   ship   110 feet   317 tons   D 12' 7"   BH
    B Kingston 1833
    R 1833 Boston (vol. 33 p. 379)
    C Ebenezer Evans
    O Charles W. Cartwright of Boston, Ebenezer Evans, EK, John Seaver of
       Kingston

Marblehead   schooner   68 feet   106 tons   D 9' 5"   BH
    B Newbury 1835
    R 1835 M'head
    C John S. Peach
    H 1838 owned by George Cloutman

Mary Kimball   barque   116 feet   372 tons   D 13' 3"   BH
> B Newbury 1835   Jackman, builder
> R 1835, 1842 M'head FT, also Newburyport 1835
> C Francis Freeto
> O EK and Francis Freeto, M'head
> H Probably named for EK's wife Mary who died in 1826. 1837 Joseph Bessom
>   drowned at sea. Carried salt from Cadiz until 1845. "Lost" after 1856

Science   schooner   53 feet   49 tons   D 6' 11"
> B Ipswich 1819
> R 1837 M'head
> C Ed Kimball
> H 1836 owned by Joseph W. Green, Richard B. Caswell, William Nutting

Mary   schooner   63 feet   81 tons   D 7' 10"
> B Amesbury 1818
> R 1837 M'head
> C Joseph Phillips
> O EK and Benj Porter of M'head
> H 1838 owned by Jon Thompson and Peter Cloutman

Philanthropist   schooner   76 feet   111 tons   D 7' 6"
> B Waldoboro, ME 1826
> R 1837 M'head
> C William Loud
> O EK, William S. and Ephraim Cloud of Orrington, Frederick Kinsell of Wal-
>   doboro, Messinger Fisher, Joseph Lambert of Bangor

Charlotte   schooner   53 feet   51 tons   D 6' 11"
> B Danvers 1820
> R 1837 M'head
> C Robert Cloutman
> O EK, Benj. Porter, Benj. Kent
> H 1823 owned by Green, Porter, Kent, Thompson

Nathaniel Hooper ship   121 feet   420 tons   D 13' 11"   BH
    B Newbury 1837
    R 1839, 1844, 1847 M'head FT, also New York 7/11/48
    C Wm. Churchill, Knott P. Bray (1847)
    O John Chandler, Francis Freeto, Benj Porter and EK
    H 1844 owned by EK, John Bubier, Porter, Wm Churchill of New York City.
       1847 owned by EK, Bubier, Porter. Carried salt from Cadiz

Jane schooner   85 feet   142 tons   D 8' 6"   BH
    B Waldoboro, ME 1833
    R 1839 M'head
    C William Loud
    O EK, Henry Flagg, Charles Thacher of Bangor, Henry Kennedy of Waldoboro,
       Judah Bartlett of Orrington, ME

John schooner   67 feet   99 tons   D 9' 3"   BH
    B Newbury 1839
    R 1839, 1840, 1842, 1843, 1844, 1845 M'head
    C Philip Bridges [Bridgeo], Hira Nickerson (1842), Ephraim Eldridge (1844)
    H Probably named for brother John d. 1835

Two Brothers schooner   73 feet   107 tons   D 7' 8"
    B Bristol, ME 1825
    R 1839, 1840, 1844 M'head
    C John S. Pitman, Jacob Elwell (1840), Amos Mitchell (1844)
    O EK and Joshua Fuller of Castine, ME. 1840 EK only

Thomas schooner   67 feet   87 tons   D 8' 1"
    B Newbury 1840
    R 1840, 1845 M'head
    C John White II, Benj. F. Weeks (1845)
    H probably named for son Thomas, lost at sea 1837

Elizabeth   schooner   63 feet   79 tons   D 7' 6"   BH
    B Essex 1836
    R 1842, 1845, 1846 M'head
    C Moses Wiley, Shadrach Small (1845), Nathan Nickerson (1846)
    O EK and Richard Girdler; 1845 EK only
    H 1842 owned by William Hammond

Atlanta   schooner   80 feet   132 tons   D 8' 1"   BH
    B Prospect, ME 1833
    R 1842 M'head
    C Philip Bridgeo

Sardius   barque   96 feet   267 tons   D 12' 6"   BH
    B New York City 1828
    R 1843 M'head FT
    C Joseph Lindsey
    O EK, Joseph Lindsey, Frederick A. Bokee of New York
        H carried salt from Cadiz

Mount Vernon   schooner   64 feet   137 tons   D 8' 1"
    B Essex 1833
    R 1845 M'head
    C Ephraim Cole
    H 1841 owned by David Blaney

President   schooner   67 feet   122 tons   D 10' 10"
    B Salisbury 1817
    R 1845 M'head
    C Philip Meservey
    H 1820 owned by Robert Hooper. 1835 owned by Broughton

Independence   schooner   60 feet   72 tons   D 8' 3"
    B Manchester 1819
    R 1846 (10/5/46) M'head
    C Philip H. White
    H May and November 1846 owned by Joseph W. Green Jr.

Wenham   bark   132 feet   523 tons
    B Newbury 1846
    R Newburyport 1847
    C Churchill
    O EK, J. Bubier, Churchill

Tyringham   barque   141 feet   608 tons   D 15' 4"   BH
    B Newbury 1848
    R Newburyport 1848, also New York 10/4/49
    C Churchill
    O EK and Churchill
    H owned by EK as late as 1859 (AL)

Robert Hooper   ship   155 feet   756 tons   D 17' 3"   W 32' 7"   BH
    B 1849 Marblehead
    R 10/31/1849 M'head FT, also Boston 1852 (vol. 52A p. 281)
    C William Churchill
    O EK 3/4 and William Churchill, NY, master mariner 1/4
    H owned by Zerega in 1853, NY 11/10/53

Compromise   ship   158 feet   794 tons   D 16' 6"   W 33'   BH
    B Marblehead 1850 Henry Ewell, master carpenter
    R 12/5/1850 M'head FT, also Boston 12/31/50, New York 10/22/53
    C Wm Churchill, John Riley
    O EK 3/4, John Riley of Dover, NH 1/4
    H sold before 1858

Anna Kimball   ship   161 feet   848 tons   D 16' 11"   W 33' 10" BH
    B Marblehead 1852   Henry T. Ewell, builder
    R 2/23/52, 1858 Boston (vol. 52 p.56, 90), also New York 11/26/56
    C Joseph Webster, Charles Marsh (1858)
    O Edmund Kimball, 1858: EK of Wenham 19/24, Charles Marsh of Newbury-
        port 3/24, Thornton B. Rennell of Philadelphia 2/24
    H Probably named for youngest daughter. Owned by Kimball & Webster as late
        as 1869 (AL)

Elizabeth Kimball   clipper ship   169 feet   997 tons   D 17' 11"   W 35' 10"
  BH   eliptical stern
  B Marblehead 1853   Benj Dutton builder
  R 12/24/53 Boston (vol. 53A pp. 515, 462), also New York 6/16/62
  C Christopher Lewis, Thomas S. Condon (1855)
  O Edmund Kimball of Wenham 7/8, and Amos Chase of Saco, ME 1/8
  H Probably named for second-youngest daughter. *c.* 1863 sold to Pope and
      Talbot.

Mary   clipper ship   179 feet   1,148 tons   D 18' 8"   W 37'   BH
  B Marblehead 1854 Benj Dutton builder
  R 12/6/1854 M'head FT
  C William Churchill, John Bridgeo
  O EK, Joseph P. Turner, Henry Pitman, 1/3 each
  H Probably named for daughter, Turner's wife. Boston to San Francisco 112 days,
      May 22–Sept 11, 1857. 1858 struck coral in Bahamas. 1862 owned by J.P.
      Turner.

Southern Belle   ship   183 feet   1,197 tons   D 18' 10"   W 37' 8"
          figurehead
  B Marblehead 1855–56   Benj. Dutton builder
  R 3/14/56 Boston (vol. 56 p. 85)
  C Christopher Lewis
  O EK 7/8, Christopher Lewis of W. Yarmouth 1/8
      H 10/17/56 caught fire and burned in the Grand Banks

Belle of the Sea   clipper ship   188 feet   1,255 tons   D 19'   W 38'
          elliptical stern
  B Marblehead 1857   Henry T. Ewell builder
  R 4/17/57 Boston (vol. 57 pp.106 and 108), also New York 1/13/63
  C Christopher Lewis, Sigsbee
  O Edmond Kimball of Beverly 7/8 and C. Lewis 1/8
  H Boston to San Francisco 128 days April 25–August 31, 1857. New York to San
      Francisco 134 days Nov 28, 1860–April 19, 1861. 1864 sold to Nickerson.

Lady Washington   ship   174 feet   1,024 tons   D 23'   W 35'   figurehead
     B Boston 1863   Benj. Dutton, master builder
     R New York 8/25/63
     C Wm P. Sigsbee
     H 2/20/64 owned by Aaron Holbrook 1/4 and John Bates 3/4

---

[1] Registry records in Marblehead, Boston, Newburyport, and New York.

Appendix D:

Chronological List of Vessels Built in Marblehead, 1800–58[1]

B   year built
R   date registered (in Marblehead unless otherwise stated)
C   captain
O   owner/s

Good Intent   schooner   34 feet   29 tons   pink stern
    B 1813   R 5/18/1815
    C Benjamin Lumbey
    O Ebenezer Tappan, Manchester

Talus   schooner   39 feet   22 tons
    B 1838   R 7/3/1838
    C James B. Topham
    O James Topham, James B. Topham, Benj. A. Robinson, Elisha P. Topham

Colonel Orne schooner   54 feet   54 tons
    B1847   R 7/19/1847
    C James B. Topham
    O James B. Topham, Elisha GT. B. Topham, James Topham, Edward B. Harris,
    James Elwell

Robert Hooper   ship 155 feet 756 tons
    B 1849   R 10/31/49
    C William Churchill
    O Edmund Kimball 3/4 and William Churchill, master mariner, New York 1/4

Compromise ship   158 feet 794 tons
    B 1850 Henry Ewell master carpenter   R 12/5/1850
    C William Churchill
    O Edmund Kimball 3/4 and John Riley of Dover, N. H. 1/4

Ariel   schooner   73 feet 104 tons
    B 1851   R 6/11/1851
    C Luther Turner
    O Joseph P. Turner 1/3, Knott Martin 2nd 1/3, Henry F. Pitman 1/3

Emeline   schooner   74 feet 107 tons
    B 1851   R 6/12/1851
    C John W. Chadwick
    O William Humphreys, Jr. 3/8, Ebenezer S. Twisden 3/8, Thomas Garney 2/8

Amy Knight   schooner   67 feet   93 tons
    B 1851   R 6/19/1851
    C Benjamin Knight
    O George Knight 1/3, William Hammond 1/3, John Proctor Jr. 1/3

Anna Kimball   ship   161 feet 848 tons
    B 1852   Henry T. Ewell builder   R Boston 2/23/52
    C Joseph Webster
    O Edmund Kimball

Marblehead   schooner   67 feet   87 tons
    B 1852   R 4/5/1852
    C Benjamin Rose
    O Henry F. Pitman 3/8, Samuel H. Brown 3/8, David L. Simpson 2/8

Boys   schooner   69 feet   94 tons
    B 1852   R 4/30/52
    C William Frost II
    O George Knight 1/4, Azor O. Knight 1/4, William Hammond 1/4, John Proctor Jr. 1/4

Rising Son   schooner   75 feet   102 tons
    B 1852   R 4/30/1852
    C Francis A. Smith
    O William Humphreys Jr. 1/2, Ebenezer S. Twisden 1/2

John Phillips schooner   77 feet   119 tons
  B 1852   R 5/4/1852
  C John Bridgeo
  O Henry F. Pitman 1/2, Joseph P. Turner 1/2

Helen   schooner   70 feet   90 tons
  B 1852   R 7/12/1852
  C Martin S. Peach
  O John Quiner 3/4, William Whippen 1/4

Sarah Jane   schooner   76 feet   112 tons
  B 1852   R 7/13/1852
  C Francis A. Smith
  O William Humphreys, Jr. 1/2, Ebenezer S. Twisden 1/2

Leo schooner   43 feet   27 tons
  B 1852   R 9/17/1853
  C William T. High
  O Thomas Snow II 7/24, S.L. and W.D. Bickford 6/24, William B. Brown 4/24,
  William H. Hooper 4/24, Edward Arnold 3/24

Blue Wave   schooner   68 feet   92 tons
  B 1853   R 4/13/1853
  C Andrew J. Bowden
  O Samuel H. Brown, shoreman 1/4, Henry F. Pitman 1/4, Joshua O. Bowden
  1/4, Andrew J. Bowden 1/4

Young America schooner   hailport NY   elliptic stern   82 feet   151 tons
  B 1853   R 5/31/1853
  C Enoch H. Ackley
  O Minor C. Story NY

Indicator   schooner   elliptic stern   98 feet   177 tons
  B 1853   R 12/21/1853
  C Franklin Augustus Gregory
  O Joseph Gregory

Elizabeth Kimball   clipper ship   elliptical stern   169 feet 997 tons
    B 1853   Benjamin Dutton, builder   R Boston 12/24/1853
    C Christopher Lewis
    O Edmund Kimball, Wenham 7/8 and Amos Chase of Saco ME 1/8

Martha and Mary   schooner   elliptical stern   72 feet   100 tons
    B 1854   R 4/20/1854
    C Samuel H. Davis
    O Knott Martin, merchant

Mary   clipper ship   179 feet 1,148 tons
    B 1854   Benjamin Dutton, builder   R 12/6/1854
    C William Churchill
    O Edmund Kimball 1/3, Joseph P. Turner 1/3, Henry Pitman 1/3

Curlew   brig   110 feet 247 tons
    B 1855   John S.M. Harris, builder R Boston 1855
    C Joseph Gregory
    O Samuel Hooper, Boston

Southern Belle   ship   183 feet 1,197 tons
    B 1856   Benjamin Dutton, builder   R Boston 3/14/1856
    C Christopher Lewis
    O Edmund Kimball 7/8, Christopher Lewis of W. Yarmouth 1/8

Philip Bridgeo   schooner   75 feet   101 tons
    B 1856   R 4/29/1856
    C Ambrose H. Meservey
    O Joseph W. Lindsey 1/2, Philip B. Lindsey 1/2

Riga   ship   elliptic stern   140 feet 586 tons
    B 1856   R 1857
    C Francis Freeto
    O Francis Freeto 1/2, William Courtiss 1/2

Belle of the Sea   clipper ship   elliptical stern   188 feet   1,255 tons
    B 1857   Henry T. Ewell, builder   R Boston 4/17/57
    C Christopher Lewis
    O Edmund Kimball of Beverly 7/8, C. Lewis 1/8

Margaret   schooner   elliptic stern   71 feet   98 tons
    B 1858   R 5/2/1858
    C Harry Snow
    O Benjamin D. Dixey, shoreman

Joseph Lindsey   schooner   70 feet   94 tons
    B 1858   R 5/12/1858
    C John Collfied
    O Joseph W. Lindsey, carpenter

Lois   schooner   elliptic stern   74 feet   103 tons
    B 1858   R 5/17/1858
    C Joshua Nickerson
    O Joshua Nickerson 1/4, Archibald Crowell 1/16, John McLennen 3/16, David Kendrick 1/16, Benjamin Craig 1/4, John Spinney 1/16, Thomas ? 1/16, Bartlett and Osgood 1/16

[1] Registry records in Marblehead and Boston

Appendix E:

Ship Itineraries, 1854–1865[1]

Cl	cleared
Arr	arrived
Sp	spoken to by another ship in transit
Unc	unconfirmed

1854

Anna Kimball	*Elizabeth Kimball*
Cl Calcutta 10/14/1853 Pike	Gap
Cl Saugor 10/17	Arr Boston 12/3 from Cadiz Lewis
Portsmouth England damage	
Gap	

1855

Anna Kimball	*Elizabeth Kimball*	*Mary*	*Tyringham*
Arr Boston 6/9 Pike from Antwerp	Cl Boston 1/3 Freeman	Cl Boston 12/30/ 1854 Churchill By Silloway, Caleb & Co.	Cl Boston 1/8 Howes
Cl Boston 6/29 Howes By Jerome Merritt	Sp 2/29 lat 29.37.8 lon 29.4	Gap	At Calcutta 6/2
Cl Batavia 11/4	At Calcutta 5/3	Cl New York 10/9/ 1855	Cl Calcutta 6/30
	Cl Calcutta 6/19		Cl Sand Heads 7/11
	Arr Boston 10/25		Arr Boston 12/26
	Cl Boston 12/7 Condon By Nath'l Winsor & Co.		

1856

Anna Kimball	Elizabeth Kimball	Mary
At Manilla 1/7 Howes	Arr San Francisco 140 days Condon	Arr San Francisco 3/9 152 days Howes
Cl Manilla 2/24	Cl San Francisco 5/21	Cl San Francisco 4/2
Cl Singapore 4/9	At Calcutta 9/23 90 days	At Calcutta 7/17 100 days
Arr New York 8/29	Cl Calcutta 11/5	Cl Calcutta 10/18
Cl New York 12/14 Rennell		

1857

Anna Kimball	Elizabeth Kimball	Mary	Riga
Sp 2/2 lat 22.3s lon 31.23 Rennell	Arr Boston 2/22 103 days Condon	Arr Boston 2/5 107 days Howes	Cl New Orleans 4/3
Sp 2/8 lat 30.8 lon 28w	Cl Boston 4/11	Cl Boston 5/22 Bridgeo	Arr Liverpool 5/15
Cl Calcutta 4/11	Arr Bombay 7/9	Arr San Francisco 9/11 109-112 days	Cl Liverpool 6/12
At Mauritius 10/12	At Calcutta 9/23	Cl San Francisco 10/3	Arr Richmond 8/4
			Arr Bordeaux 10/20
			Cl Bordeaux 12/4

Belle of the Sea
Cl Boston 4/24
Lewis

Arr San Francisco
8/31 126 days

Cl San Francisco
9/1

1858

Anna Kimball	*Elizabeth Kimball*	*Mary*	*Belle of the Sea*
Arr Boston 1/22 Rennell	Cl Bombay 2/5 Condon	Cl Calcutta 2/2 83 days Bridgeo	Arr Calcutta 1/23 Lewis
Remetalled	At Calcutta 4/13	Arr London 5/27	Cl Calcutta 3/9
Cl Boston 4/8 Marsh	Cl Calcutta 7/4 Webb	114 days	Sp 4/3 lat 19.21s lon 1.22
At London 5/6-29	Condon dies 7/27	Cadiz 8/-	Arr London 6/19
At Shields 6/5	Cl Singapore 8/26	Boston	Cl London 9/7
Cl Liverpool 6/16	Arr Boston 12/19		Off Portland 9/15
Arr New York 7/29			Arr Melbourne 12/18
Cl New York 9/10			
At Rio 11/14			
Cl Rio 12/11			

1859

Anna Kimball	*Elizabeth Kimball*	*Mary*	*Belle of the Sea*
Cl New Orleans 4/9 Merrill	Cl Boston 1/26 WH Wilson By J. Silloway & Co.	Arr New Orleans 2/4 Bridgeo	Cl Melbourne 2/17 Lewis
At Liverpool 6/18	Arr New Orleans 4/3	Cl New Orleans 3/20	Arr Calcutta 6/17
Cl Liverpool 8/3	Cl New Orleans 5/6	At Havre 4/13	Cl Calcutta 8/8
At Rio 10/4	Arr Liverpool 6/18	Cl Havre 5/22	Arr Boston 12/1
Cl Rio 11/23	Cl Liverpool 7/14	Arr New York 6/23	
	Arr New York 8/27	Cl Mobile 10/13	
	Cl New Orleans 12/17	Arr Liverpool 11/28	

1860

Anna Kimball	*Elizabeth Kimball*	*Mary*	*Belle of the Sea*
Arr New Orleans 1/11 Marsh	Arr Liverpool 1/17 Wilson	Cl Liverpool 1/9 Bridgeo	Cl Boston 1/30 Lewis By Loring and French
Cl London 2/1	Cl Liverpool 5/22	At New Orleans 3/14	Arr New Orleans 3/16
At Yarmouth 2/7	Sp 5/24 off Bardsey	Cl New Orleans 3/31	Cl New Orleans 5/4
Arr Shields 2/27	Arr Melbourne 9/11	arr Havre 5/25	Sp 5/17 lat 34 lon 74 ½
Cl Shields 3/24	Cl Melbourne 10/18	cl Havre 6/10	At Liverpool 6/18
Passed Deal 3/30	At Newcastle NSW 10/26	arr New York 7/23 206 passengers	Cl Liverpool 7/23
In New York 5/8		cl New York 8/22	At Boston 9/4
Cl New York 7/6		aground Bahama bank	Cl Boston Janvrin
At Helvoet 8/6		arr New Orleans 9/22	Arr New York 9/28
At Rotterdam 9/2		cl New Orleans 12/9	Cl New York 11/28 Sigsbee
Arr Sunderland 9/14			
Cl Sunderland 9/28			
Passed Dungeness 9/30			
At Bermuda 11/20			

1861

Anna Kimball
Arr New York 1/26
Marsh

Cl New York 4/11

Sp 5/22 lat 12 lon 35

Cl Melbourne 8/31

Cl Otago NZ 10/-

Arr Melbourne 10/27

Cl Melbourne 12/21

Elizabeth Kimball
At Callao 1/28
Wilson

At Chinchas 3/13 loading 4/13

Cl Callao 5/1

At Valparaiso 6/4 distress

Cl Valparaiso 6/23

Arr London 9/17

Cl London 10/21 passed Deal 10/25

Arr Boston 11/19

Cl Boston 12/28 Harrison

Mary
Arr Havre 1/13
Bridgeo

Cl Havre 1/27

Arr New Orleans 3/10

Cl New Orleans 4/4

Sp 4/25 lat 41.45 lon 48.11

Sp 5/6 lat 50 ½ lon 14 ½

Arr Havre 5/19

Cl Havre 6/4

Arr Cadiz 6/19

Cl Cadiz 7/11

Arr Boston 8/23

Cl Boston 9/12

Cl New York 9/29

Arr Havre 10/24

Cl Havre

Belle of the Sea
Sp 1/1 lat 7n lon 26.11 Sigsbee

Arr San Francisco 4/18 139 days

Cl San Francisco 6/25

Arr New York 10/9 106 days

1862

Anna Kimball	*Elizabeth Kimball*	*Mary*	*Belle of the Sea*
Cl Melbourne 2/14 Marsh	Sp 1/6 lat 13.40 lon 39.43 Harrison	Arr New York 1/20 Bridgeo	Cl New York 1/3 Sigsbee
Arr Otago NZ 3/7	At Liverpool 2/6	At Boston 2/- sold to Turner	Sp 1/31 lat 25.8 lon 25.45
Cl Otago 4/15	Cl Liverpool 3/5	Cl Boston 3/12	Sp 3/14 lat 55.42 lon 70.15s
Cl Honolulu 6/7	Arr Boston 4/6	Sp 6/24 lat 46.32 lon 81.56	131 days to SF
Cl Vancouver –	Cl New York 6/19 Grindle	Arr San Francisco 8/25 165 days	Cl San Francisco 7/16
At Sydney NSW 11/10	At Shanghae 12/26 unc	Cl San Francisco 9/17	Arr New York 11/7 117 days
Cl Sydney 12/21		Arr Singapore 11/11 cl 11/17 Arr Calcutta 12/11	

1863

Anna Kimball	*Elizabeth Kimball*	*Mary*	*Belle of the Sea*
Arr Calcutta 3/8 Marsh	Cl Shanghae 2/14 Grindle	Cl Calcutta 1/17 Bridgeo	Cl New York 1/17 Foster
Ashore in Diamond Harbor 3/10	At Hong Kong 2/28	Arr London 5/13	Put back to New York 1/24
Cl Calcutta 5/13	Cl Hong Kong 4/15	Cl London 8/-	Cl New York 3/8
At Algoa Bay SA 7/17	Arr San Francisco 6/10 52 days	Arr Cardiff 8/-	Sp 5/7 lat 4.27 lon 29.30
Arr Dundee 9/27	Sold to Pope & Talbot	Cl Cardiff 9/2	Cl San Francisco 10/5 150 days to SF
Cl Dundee 11/16 Perkins put back to Dundee 11/17		Arr Gibraltar 10/19	
		At Gibraltar 10/28	
		At Cadiz 12/4	

1864

Anna Kimball	*Mary*	*Belle of the Sea*
Cl Shields 5/6 Moore	Cl Cadiz 1/1 Bridgeo	Arr Liverpool 2/20 Foster
Arr Boston 6/23	Arr St. Thomas	Gap
Cl Boston 9/26	Arr Boston	Sold
Sp 10/29 lat 8 lon 24	Sold	
Arr Buenos Aires 11/30		
At Montevideo 12/14 disg.		

1865

Anna Kimball
Cl Montevideo
1/11 Moore

Arr Turks Is. 4/16

Arr Boston 5/15

Cl Boston 9/6
Williams By WH
Kinsman & Co.

Cl St. John N.B.
10/5

Arr London 11/6
unc.

[1] Principally from the *Boston Shipping List*. Dates may not agree with other sources. Passage time principally from Howe & Matthews. Captains from best available sources.

Appendix F:

"Disasters, &c," Boston Shipping List, September 26, 1857

Queenstown,[1] Aug 31:The *Western Star*, Hammond, from Rangoon for Falmouth, E, which put in here yesterday, very leaky, after being in contact, has gone into dry dock, to discharge cargo and repair. Previous to going in, men were employed constantly at the pumps to keep her afloat, as her cutwater was carried away and several planks in her bottom were started. The collision occurred at 2 AM 30th, with an unknown vessel off the Old Head of Kinsale, and the *Western Star* went right over her, sending her to the bottom with every person on board. So sudden was the occurrence, the two vessels meeting in the dark, that the crew of the *Western Star* could only make out that the other was a bark, but could ascertain nothing of where she was from, or to what nation her crew belonged, except that some of the latter who were on deck when she struck, appeared to be neither American nor English. The captain of a Genoese ship, which ar yesterday, thinks that the vessel lost was from his country.

Tralee, Aug 31: To-day 42 bales cotton were recovered from the *Lexington*, from New Orleans for Liverpool, ashore in Brandon Bay. A heavy surf was on, and great difficulty was experienced in boarding the vessel.

Cork, Aug 31: The *Roebuck*, Soule, from Swansea to Caldera, which put in here Aug 29, and the *Western Star*, Hammond, from Rangoon for Falmouth, which put in Aug 30, both leaky, have been ordered to discharge.

The *Roebuck* had rolled and labored heavily during a gale 23d, when it was suddenly discovered that she was making five inches water per hour: set the pumps to work, and kept the crew at them, but the leak increased to nine inches, the wind having freshened. On reaching lon 12 W, the crew came aft and said they did not consider it safe for the ship to continue the voyage, upon which Capt Soule consulted with the mates and the carpenter, and resolved to make for the nearest port, and reached Cork 29th.

Bark *JW Blodget*, from Turks Island for New York, which was ashore near New Inlet bar, was got off 15th inst, by steamer *Henrietta*, and towed to Wilmington NC. She is leaky and must discharge to repair.

Foreign bark *Maria Protalanga*, from Belize, Hond, for Cork, was totally lost on the Northern Triangles, about Aug 17.

Bark *John Parker*, of Providence, from New Orleans for Rotterdam, was lost near Cape Lookout. Crew saved. The *JP* cld at New Orleans Aug 8, with 550 hhds tobacco and 7,300 staves, valued at $60,000. She was 392 tons, built at Medford in 1845, by Messrs Bramhall & Howe of Boston, and now owned by Mr S Mauran 2d, and others of Providence. Vessel believed to be insured in Boston, and freight money in Providence.

Sch *Wake*, O'Brien, from Wilmington, NC, of and for N York, sank at Ocracoke in the recent gale. The vessel is a total loss. Part of her cargo will probably be saved. The *Wake* is valued at $13,000.

Bark *Oceanus*, Adams, at Surinam from Gloucester, experienced a severe gale, no date, lat 9½, lon 52, in which she was thrown on her beams ends and had to cut away the main and mizzen masts before she righted. She arrived at Surinam with only the foremast and bowsprit left, and was so badly damaged about the hull that she would probably be condemned.

Sch *Julia Ann*, Staples, from Elizabethport, with coal, went ashore at Chatham 18th inst, and is full of water.

Sch *New Republic*, from Philadelphia for Wilmington, NC, ashore at New Inlet is a total loss. About two-thirds of the cargo has been saved in good condition, and carried over the beach to two small vessels inside, which will take it to town. The remainder would probably be saved in a damaged state.

Sch *Emily Ward*, of and for New York from Charleston, sunk at New Inlet bar, is in 10 ft water: vessel and cargo a total loss.

Sch *Abdel Kader*, of and for New York from Wilmington, NC, wrecked near New Inlet, will be a total loss: part of cargo will be saved.

Sch *Albion*, from Calais for Philadelphia, with lumber was ashore on the point of Sandy Hook, 19th to 20th inst, and will be a total loss. There is no insurance on vessel or cargo.

Sch *Lucinda Jane*, (of St George Me) Ward, fm Philadelphia for Belfast, in a sinking condition was fallen in with 18th inst, Sandy Hook NW 50 miles by sch *Anna Gardiner*, fm Philadelphia of and for Boston, which took off the captain and crew and carried them to New York 20th. The *Lucinda Jane* had been run down by an unknown brig a short time previously.

Sch *Eleanor*, Hosmer, of and from Philadelphia with lumber, went ashore prev to 20th inst, on the point of Sandy Hook, and will be a total loss: crew saved. The *Eleanor* is an A2 vessel of 159 tons, built at Lincolnville in 1856. At last accounts the vessel lay high upon and nearly broadside on the beach, with both mast gone.

Brig *Virginia*, of and from Mobile, at Belize, Hond, had been ashore at Omoa in a gale, sunk, and was pumped out at a very heavy expense. On arrival at B her funds were exhausted and she lay on the beach at St Georges Bay, 18th ult, full of water.

Brig *Albion Cooper*, of and from Portland for Havana burned at sea, was a poor vessel of 185 tons, rating A3, built at Pittston, Me, in 1845, valued at not over $3,000. She was owned by Messrs Whittier, Waterhouse and Dyer, of Portland, and the captain, D R Humphrey, of Falmouth. The mate, Mr Smith, also belongs to Portland. The cargo is fully insured at the Dean Insurance Office in Portland, and there is also an insurance of $600 on the freight.

Sp brig *Luzon*, from Havana for Falmouth, with sugar and molasses, went ashore near New Topsail Inlet, NC, in the gale night of 12th inst, and with her cargo was expected to be a total loss.

Sch *New Republic*, of and from Philadelphia for Wilmington, NC, went on the beach at New Topsail Inlet morn of 13th inst.

A despatch from Norfolk, dated 22d inst, states that the bark *Cuba*, from Wilmington, NC, for Surinam, is off Ocracoke, dismasted. The captain was at Norfolk for assistance. A bark, name unknown, was ashore at Ocracoke and Beaufort. Sch *C. M'Clees*, and other vessels, names unknown, are ashore off Beaufort. Sch *E S Willett* has broken in two.

Bark *Fame*, (of Richmond) Kennedy, from Rio Janeiro about Aug 15 for Baltimore, with 6,600 bags coffee, had a heavy gale 10th inst, off Cape Lookout, which soon increased to a hurricane.[2] On the morning of 12th, off Cape Fear, while lying to under close reefed main topsail, was thrown on her beam ends, had everything from off deck washed overboard, and was obliged to cut away foremast, which, together with main topgallantmast, sails, and everything attached, were lost. On Monday night, to the northward of Cape Hatteras, exchanged signals with a ship, which had lost foretopmast and main topgallantmast; supposed to be the *Banshee*, from Rio Janeiro for Batimore.

Steamer *Joseph Whitney*, at this port, from Baltimore on 14th inst, at 2 PM, between Smith's and Hog Islands, picked up three small boats containing the passengers and most of the officers and crew of the steamer *Norfolk*, (formerly the *Penobscot*) Kelley, from Philadelphia for Norfolk, which had been abandoned 9 hours previously. The *Norfolk* went to pieces in the violent NE gale on Sunday night, 10 miles SE of Chincoteague. The passengers saved numbered 40. They were landed at Delaware Breakwater on Tuesday.

Ship *M de Embil*, of Bath, Stephen Albee, of Wiscasset, master, (with wife and child on board) sailed from New York 29th December last, with a cargo of grain for Santander, Spain, and has not since been heard from. She probably foundered at sea in a severe gale which occurred shortly after she sailed. The *M de Embil* was a first class ship of 500 tons built in 1852. She is insured in Bath for $20,000.

Brig *Vermont*, of Newport, RI, wrecked on Western Head, 16th inst, on the passage from Pictou for Boston, was an A2½ vessel, of 170 tons, built at Ellsworth, Me, in 1851, owned in Newport, RI, and valued at about $5,000.

Ship *Floating Zephyr*, (of Boston) Young, from Pensacola about Aug 15 for Buenos Ayres, was abandoned, no date, after being waterlogged in the late gale. Her officers and crew were put on board a Charleston pilot boat, from ship *Florida*, from Liverpool for Savannah, which called of Charleston 19th. The *F Z* was 645 tons, rated A1½, was built at Bristol, Me, in 1853, and owned by Messrs Blanchard & Sherman.

Bark *John Parker*, was valued at $14,000 and insured in Boston for $12,000—7,000 at the Boston Insurance Co, and 5,000 at the Mercantile Marine. Her freight money was insured in Providence for $6,000—equally divided between the American and Gaspee offices. Cargo insured in Europe.

A three masted sch, badly wrecked, steering N, under close reefed fore and mainsail, the other sails apparently gone, was passed 14th inst, lat 35½, lon 73, by sch *E S Janes*, at Philadelphia. She was deeply laden, painted lead color, with no boat, spanker boom, cutwater, galley, or midship house; bulwarks gone, water breaking across the deck; she wanted no assistance. Could not make out her name.

The brig which was in contact with sch *Lucinda Jane*, of St George, Me, from Philadelphia for Belfast, before reported abandoned, was understood to be bound to Charleston or

Jacksonville. Capt Wall reports that when he found that his sch was sinking, he requested the brig to lie by her, but the captain refused, saying "I would help you to h__l if I had a chance." The *Lucinda Jane* was built in Waldoboro in 1852, 130 tons, and rated A2.

Brig *Borneo*, Craig, from New York for Jacksonville, put back 21st, having been run into on the 18th, 30 miles East of Squan, by sch *Lucinda Jane*, of St George, from Philadelphia for Belfast, (before reported), which carried away all the main weather gear, with fore topgallant mast, and split mainmast.

Liverpool, Sept 7: The *Alfred Storer*, Comery, from Bombay which arrived here yesterday, encountered a hurricane from SW to NW, Aug 25, in lat 38 N, lon 94^3 W, which threw her on her beam ends for several hours, and carried away her sails.

Deal, Sept 5: The Am bark *Asa Sawyer*, Gates, for Rio Janeiro, in working out of the Downs this morning, found the *Pactolus*, Turney, at anchor, and did her some damage that will take a few days to repair.

Cork, Sept 5: The Am ship *Western Star*, has discharged cargo into the bonded stores of the Royal Victoria Dockyard, and hauled into a dry dock for repairs.

Castle Gregory, Sept 5: All the cotton is landed from the wrecked ship *Lexington*, consisting of 1,088 bales, and about 50 bales loose cotton; 6,000 staves have also been got ashore; weather favorable.

Steamship *Central America*, from Aspinwall for New York, foundered 12th inst. Upwards of 400 lives were lost.[4]

[1] Now Cobh, near Cork, Ireland.

[2] The hurricane of September 11, 1857, in North Carolina, #65 on the National Weather Service list of Atlantic cyclones with more than 25 deaths, caused 424 deaths.

[3] Probably 74 W (at latitude 38 N, the longitude of 94 W is in western Missouri, more than 550 miles from the sea)

[4] The story of this wreck and the 1987 recovery of its gold cargo is told in Kinder (1998).

Bibliography

Adams, Charles Francis, *Richard Henry Dana, a Biography*, Boston: Houghton Mifflin and Co., 1890

Albion, Robert Greenhalgh, *Square-Riggers on Schedule: The New York Sailing Packets to England, France, and the Cotton Ports*, Princeton: Princeton University Press, 1938; reprinted, Hamden, CT: Archon, 1965

Albion, Robert Greenhalgh, *The Rise of New York Port, 1815-1860,* New York: Charles Scribner's Sons, 1939

Albury, Paul, *The Story of the Bahamas*, New York: St. Martin's Press, 1976

Anson, Peter F., *Mariners of Brittany*, New York: Dutton, 1931; reprinted, London: Dent, 1974

Baehre, Rainer K., *Outrageous Seas: Shipwreck and Survival in the Waters off Newfoundland, 1583–1893*, Montreal and Kingston: McGill-Queen's University Press, 1999

Bayley, William H., and Oliver O. Jones, *History of the Marine Society of Newburyport*, Newburyport, MA: Daily News, 1906

Beasley, W.G., *The Modern History of Japan*, New York: Praeger, 1963; reprinted, New York: St. Martin's Press, 1981

Bentley, Rev. William, *The Diary of William Bentley, D.D., Pastor of the East Church, Salem, Massachusetts*, 4 vols, Salem: Essex Institute, 1905–14; reprinted, Gloucester, MA: Smith, 1962

Bigelow, Henry B., and William W. Welsh, *Fishes of the Gulf of Maine*, Caldwell, NJ: Blackburn Press, 1925

Billias, George Athan, *General John Glover and his Marblehead Mariners*, New York: Holt, 1960

Binney, C.J.F., *The History and Genealogy of the Prentice, or Prentiss, Family in New England, from 1631 to 1852,* Boston: privately printed, 1852

Blunt, Joseph, *The Shipmaster's Assistant and Commercial Digest*, New York: E. and G.W. Blunt, 1837

Bourne, Russell, *The View from Front Street: Travels through New England's Historic Fishing Communities*, New York: Norton, 1989

Boston Looks Seaward, The Story of the Port 1630-1940, Workers of the Writers' Program of the Work Projects Administration in the State of Massachusetts, Boston: Bruce Humphries, Inc., 1941, reprinted 1970.

Bowden, William Hammond, "The Commerce of Marblehead: 1665–1775," *Essex Institute Historical Collections* (1932): 117ff.

Bradlee, Francis B.C., *Marblehead's Foreign Commerce, 1789–1850*, Salem: Essex Institute, 1929

Brewington, Dorothy E.R., *Dictionary of Marine Artists,* Salem: Peabody Museum, and Mystic, CT: Mystic Seaport Museum, 1982

Brewington, Dorothy E.R., *Marine Paintings and Drawings in the Mystic Seaport Museum*, Mystic, CT: Mystic Seaport Museum, 1982

Browne, Benjamin Frederick, "Papers of an old [Dartmoor] Prisoner," chapter 3, *United States Democratic Review* 91 (January 1846): 31ff.; republished as *The Yarn of a Yankee Privateer*, New York: Funk and Wagnall, 1926

Cadigan, Sean, "Marine Resource Exploitation and Development: Historical Antecedents in the Debate over Technology and Ecology in the Newfoundland Fishery, 1815-1855," in *Marine Resources and Human Societies in the North Atlantic Since 1500*, Institute of Social and Economic Research, Memorial University of Newfoundland (1995) (ISER Conf. Pap. No. 5)

Chadwick, John W., "Marblehead," *Harpers New Monthly Magazine* 49 (July 1874): 181-202

Chadwick, John W., "Old Marblehead," *New England Magazine* 18 (July 1895): 611-628

Chadwick, John W., *Cap'n Chadwick, Marblehead Skipper and Shoemaker*, Boston: American Unitarian Association, 1906

Chapelle, Howard I., *The American Fishing Schooners, 1825–1935*, New York: Norton, 1973

Cheney, Robert K., *Maritime History of the Merrimac*, Newburyport: Newburyport Press, Inc., 1964

Clark, Arthur H., *The Clipper Ship Era*, New York: Putnam, 1910

Clark, George R., *et al.*, *A Short History of the United States Navy*, Philadelphia: Lippincott, 1911; reprinted, 1939

Connolly, James B., *Master Mariner: The Life and Voyages of Amasa Delano*, Garden City, NY: Doubleday, 1943

Crothers, William L., *The American-Built Clipper Ship, 1850–1856: Characteristics, Construction, and Details*, Camden, ME: International Marine, 1997

Cutler, Carl C., *Greyhounds of the Sea: The Story of the American Clipper Ship*, New York: Putnam, 1930; 3rd edition, Annapolis, MD: Naval Institute Press, 1984

Cutler, Carl C., *Queens of the Western Ocean: The Story of America's Mail and Passenger Sailing Lines*, Annapolis, MD: Naval Institute Press, 1961

Daggett, Kendrick Price, *Fifty Years of Fortitude: The Maritime Career of Captain Jotham Blaisdell of Kennebunk, Maine, 1810–1860*, Mystic, CT: Mystic Seaport Museum, 1988

Dana, Richard Henry, Jr., *Two Years Before the Mast and Twenty-four Years After,* 1840

Dean, Nicholas, *Snow Squall: The Last American Clipper Ship*, Gardiner, ME: Tilbury House, and Bath, ME: Maine Maritimes Museum, 2001

Doeringer, Peter B., Philip I. Moss, and David G. Terkla, *The New England Fishing Economy: Jobs, Income, and Kinship*, Amherst: University of Massachusetts Press, 1986

Douglass, William, *A Summary, Historical and Political, of the First Planting, Progressive Improvements, and Present State of the British Settlements in North America*, 2 vols, Boston: Rogers and Fowle, 1749–52

Drake, Samuel Adams, *Nooks and Corners of the New England Coast,* New York: Harper, 1875; reprinted, Detroit: Singing Tree Press, 1969

Drinker, Sandwith, *A Private Journal of Events and Scenes at Sea and in India*, Boston: 1990

Dun and Co., *Massachusetts* and *New York*, R. G. Dun & Co. Collection, Baker Library, Harvard Business School, Cambridge, MA

Dunne, Gerald T., *Justice Joseph Story and the Rise of the Supreme Court*, New York: Simon and Schuster, 1970

Dwight, Timothy, *Travels in New England and New York* (1821–22), 4 vols, edited by Barbara Miller Solomon, Cambridge, MA: Belknap Press, 1969

Faler, Paul G., *Mechanics and Manufacturers in the Early Industrial Revolution: Lynn, Massachusetts, 1780–1860,* Albany: State University of New York Press, 1981

Flanders, Henry, *A Treatise on Maritime Law*, Boston: Little, Brown, 1852; reprinted, Union, NJ: Lawbook Exchange

Forbes, Abner, and J.W. Greene, *Our First Men, or a Catalogue of the Richest Men of Massachusetts*, Boston: W.V. Spencer, 1851

"From Judicial Grant to Legislative Power: The Admiralty Clause in the Nineteenth Century," *Harvard Law Review* 1214 (1954)

German, Andrew W., "History of the Early Fisheries, 1720–1930," in *Georges Bank*, edited by Richard H. Backus, Cambridge, MA: MIT Press, 1987

Girdler, L. Tracy, *An Antebellum Life at Sea,* Montgomery, AL: Black Belt Press, 1997

Gosnell, Harpur Allen, *Before the Mast in the Clippers: The Diaries of Charles A. Abbey, 1856 to 1860*, New York: Dover, 1989

Gray, Thomas E., *The Founding of Marblehead*, Baltimore, MD: Gateway Press, 1984

Greenlaw, Linda, *The Hungry Ocean*, New York: Hyperion, 1999.

Harlow, Alvin F., *Old Post Bags: The Story of the Sending of a Letter in Ancient and Modern Times*, New York: D. Appleton, 1928

Harris, Leslie, "Seeking Equilibrium: An Historical Glance at Aspects of the Newfoundland Fisheries," in *The Newfoundland Groundfish Fisheries: Defining the Reality*, edited by K. Storey, St. John's: Memorial University Institute of Social and Economic Research, 1993 (ISER Conf. Proc. 1993)

Hazard, Blanche Evans, *The Organization of the Boot and Shoe Industry in Massachusetts before 1875*, Cambridge, MA: Harvard University Press, 1921; reprinted, New York: A.M. Kelley, 1969

Heyrman, Christine Leigh, *Commerce and Culture; The Maritime Communities of Colonial Massachusetts, 1690-1750,* New York: W.W. Norton, 1984.

Hidy, Ralph W., *The House of Baring in American Trade and Finance: English Merchant Bankers at Work, 1763–1861*, Cambridge, MA: Harvard University Press, 1949; reprinted, New York: Russell and Russell, 1970

Hind, Henry Youle, *Explorations in the Interior of the Labrador Peninsula, the Country of the Montagnais and Nasquapee Indians*, London: Longman, Green 1863; reprinted, Millwood, NY: Kraus Reprint, 1973

Howe, Octavius T., M.D., and Frederick C. Matthews, *American Clipper Ships, 1833–1858*, 2 vols, Salem: Marine Research Society, 1926; reprinted, New York: Dover, 1986

Hutchings, Jeffrey A., "Spatial and Temporal Variation in the Exploitation of Northern Cod, Gadus Morhua: A Historical Perspective from 1500 to Present," in *Marine Resources and Human Societies in the North Atlantic Since 1500*, Institute of Social and Economic Research, Memorial University of Newfoundland (1995) (ISER Conf. Pap. No. 5)

Hutchins, John Greenwood Brown, *American Maritime Industries and Public Policy, 1789–1914: An Economic History*, Cambridge, MA: Harvard University Press, 1941; reprinted, New York: Russell and Russell, 1969

Innis, Harold A., *The Cod Fisheries: The History of an International Economy*, New Haven, CT: Yale University Press, 1940; revised edition, Toronto: University of Toronto Press, 1978

Irving, Washington, *The Sketch Book of Geoffrey Crayon, Gent.*, 1835

Janzen, Olaf U., "The Fishery and Fish Trade, 1500–1800," in *A Reader's Guide to the History of Newfoundland and Labrador to 1869*, www.swgc.mun.ca/nfld%5Fhistory/nfld%5Fhistory%5Ffishery.htm

Johnson, David N., "The Shoemaker's Kit," from his *Sketches of Lynn*, Lynn, MA: T.P. Nichols, 1880; reprinted, Westport, CT: Greenwood, 1970

Junger, Sebastian, *The Perfect Storm*, New York: W.W. Norton & Co., 1997, reprinted by HarperPaperbacks, 1998

Karr, Ronald Dale, *The Rail Lines of Southern New England: A Handbook of Railroad History*, Pepperell, MA: Branch Line Press, 1995

Kinder, Gary, *Ship of Gold in the Deep Blue Sea*, New York: Atlantic Monthly Press, 1998

Kindleberger, Charles P., *Manias, Panics, and Crashes: A History of Financial Crises*, New York: Basic Books, 1978; 4th edition, New York: Wiley, 2000

Kipling, *Captains Courageous*, New York: Grosset & Dunlop, 1896

Kittredge, Henry C., *Shipmasters of Cape Cod*, Boston and New York: Houghton Mifflin, 1935; reprinted, Hamden, CT: Archon Books, 1971

Laing, Alexander, *American Ships*, New York: American Heritage Press, 1971

Larcom, Lucy, *A New England Girlhood, Outlined from Memory*, Boston and New York: Houghton Mifflin, 1889; reprinted, Boston: Northeastern University Press, 1986

Lindsey, Benjamin J., *Old Marblehead Sea Captains and the Ships in Which They Sailed*, Marblehead: Marblehead Historical Society, 1915

Lord, Priscilla Sawyer, and Virginia Clegg Gamage, *Marblehead: The Spirit of '76 Lives Here*, Philadelphia: Chilton, 1972

Loti, Pierre, *An Iceland Fisherman*, translated by Anna Farwell de Koven, Chicago: A.C. McClurg, 1890

Lyon, Jane D., *Clipper Ships and Captains*, New York: American Heritage, 1962

McFarland, Raymond, *A History of the New England Fisheries*, New York: D. Appleton (for University of Pennsylvania), 1911

MacGregor, David R., *The Tea Clippers, Their History and Development 1833-75*, London: Conway Maritime Press Ltd. (1983)

Maclay, Edgar S., *A History of American Privateers*, New York: D. Appleton, 1899; reprinted, Freeport, NY: Books for Libraries Press, 1970

Magnusson, Gudmundur, "Fishing and Living: The Icelandic Experience," in *The New-foundland Groundfish Fisheries: Defining the Reality*, edited by K. Storey, St. John's: Memorial University Institute of Social and Economic Research, 1993 (ISER Conf. Proc. 1993)

Marblehead Messenger, "A Brief History of the National Grand Bank," Thursday April 29, 1965, p. 10

Maritime Heritage Project, California, www.maritimeheritage.org/import

Melville, Herman, *Redburn: His First Voyage*, 1849

Morison, Samuel Eliot, *The Maritime History of Massachusetts, 1783–1860*, Boston and New York: Houghton Mifflin, 1921; reprinted, Boston: Northeastern University Press, 1979

Morison, Samuel Eliot, *"Old Bruin": Commodore Matthew C. Perry, 1794–1858*, Boston: Little Brown, 1967

Morrison, Leonard Allison, and Stephen Pasehall Sharples, *History of the Kimball Family in America, from 1634 to 1897*, Boston: Damrell and Upham, 1897; revised edition, edited by Judith A. Kimball and George H. Kimball, Kittery, ME: privately printed, 1988

Mudgett, Kathryn, "'Cruelty to Seamen': Richard Henry Dana Jr., Justice Story, and the Case of Nichols and Couch," *American Neptune* 47 (2002)

Newmyer, R. Kent, *Supreme Court Justice Joseph Story, Statesman of the Old Republic*, Chapel Hill: University of North Carolina Press, 1985

Nielsen, J. Rasmus, and Michael Andersen, "Feeding Habits and Density Patterns of Greenland Cod … Compared to Those of the Coexisting Atlantic Cod …," *Journal of Northwest Atlantic Fishery Science* 29 (2001): 1–22 (also available online at www.nafo.ca/publications/journal/j29/nielsen.pdf)

Northeast Fisheries Science Center, *Final Report of Working Group on Re-Evaluation of Biological Reference Points for Northeast Groundfish*, 2002, CRD02-04

Pope, Charles Henry and Hooper, Thomas, *Hooper Genealogy*, Boston: C.H. Pope, 1908

Porter, Joseph Whitcomb, *A Genealogy of the Descendants of Richard Porter… also Some Account of the Descendants of John Porter*, Bangor, ME: Burr and Robinson, 1878

Reynolds, Joseph, *Peter Gott, the Cape Ann Fisherman*, Boston: Jewett, and New York: Sheldon, Blakeman, 1856

Roads, Samuel, Jr. *The History and Traditions of Marblehead*, 3rd edition: Marblehead: N.A. Lindsey, 1897

Rowe, William H., *Maritime History of Maine: Three Centuries of Shipbuilding and Seafaring*, New York: Norton, 1948; reprinted, Gardiner, ME: Harpswell Press, 1989

Ryan, Shannon, *Fish out of Water, the Newfoundland Saltfish Trade 1814–1914*, St John's, Newfoundland: Breakwater Books, 1986

Serchuk, Fredric M., and Susan E. Wigley, "Assessment and Management of the Georges Bank Cod Fishery: An Historical Review and Evaluation," *Journal of Northwest Atlantic Fishery Science* (1992): 25–52

Shaw, David A., *Flying Cloud: The True Story of America's Most Famous Clipper Ship and the Woman who Guided Her*, New York: Morrow, 2000

Sprague, Peleg, *Decisions of Hon. Peleg Sprague, in Admiralty and Maritime Causes, in the District Court of the United States for the District of Massachusetts 1841–1864*, vol. 1, edited by F.E. Parker, 1861; vol. 2, edited by John Lathrop, 1865, Philadelphia: T. and J.W. Johnson

Stampp, Kenneth M., *America in 1857: A Nation on the Brink*, New York: Oxford University Press, 1990

Standage, Tom, *The Victorian Internet: The Remarkable Story of the Telegraph and the Nineteenth Century's On-Line Pioneers*, New York: Walker, 1998

Story, Dana A., *Shipbuilders of Essex: A Chronicle of Yankee Endeavour*, Gloucester, MA: Ten Pound Island, 1995

Story, Joseph, *Life and Letters of Joseph Story, Associate Justice of the Supreme Court of the United States, and Dane Professor of Law at Harvard University*, edited by William W. Story, 2 vols, Boston: Little, Brown, 1851; reprinted, Union, NJ: Lawbook Exchange, 2000

"Temperence," Fifth Annual Report of the New York State Society for the Promotion of Temperance, 39 *North American Review* 85, 494-532 (1834)

Tutt, Richard, "Marblehead and its Fisheries" in *A Collection of Historical Papers on Old Marblehead*, Abbott Public Library, Marblehead (unpublished typescript)

Vickers, Daniel, *Farmers and Fishermen: Two Centuries of Work in Essex County, Massachusetts, 1630–1850*, Chapel Hill, NC: University of North Carolina Press, 1994

Vickers, Daniel, "Introduction," in *Marine Resources and Human Societies in the North Atlantic Since 1500*, Institute of Social and Economic Research, Memorial University of Newfoundland (1995)

Viele, John, *The Florida Keys*, vol. 3: *The Wreckers*, Sarasota, FL: Pineapple Press, 2001

Vital Records of Marblehead, Massachusetts, to the End of the Year 1849, two volumes, Salem: Essex Institute, 1903

Weightman, Gavin, *The Frozen Water Trade: A True Story*, New York: Hyperion, 2003

Wells, W.V., "Fishing Adventures on the Newfoundland Banks," *Harper's New Monthly Magazine* 130 (March 1861): 456-471

Whidden, John D., *Ocean Life in the Old Sailing-Ship Days: From Forecastle to Quarterdeck*, Boston: Little, Brown, 1908

Whipple, A.B.C., *Famous Pirates of the New World*, New York: Random House, 1958

Whipple, A.B.C., *The Challenge*, New York: Morrow, 1987

Wilkshire, Mike, "19th Century French Fishery" in *The French Presence in Newfoundland*, www.heritage.nf.ca/exploration/fpres_19th.html (1998)

"Wreckage," *Living Age* 440 (October 23, 1852): 174-178

Index